MORTON F. MELTZER is manager of the
Technical Information Center at
Martin Marietta Corporation, Orlando
division.

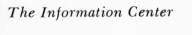

The Information Center

About the Author

MORTON F. MELTZER, manager of the Technical Information Center at Martin Marietta Corporation, Orlando division, has been in the aerospace industry for more than ten years. He earned a Bachelor of Science degree, summa cum laude, at Boston University and a Master of Business Administration at Rollins College. Mr. Meltzer is a member of the American Documentation Institute, American Library Association, and Special Libraries Association. In addition to managing the information center at Martin Marietta, he recently assisted on Project Lex for the Department of Defense, helping to prepare its *Technical Thesaurus,* and also assisted in the preparation of the Engineers Joint Council *Thesaurus of Engineering Terms.*

Morton F. Meltzer

The Information Center

Management's Hidden Asset

American Management Association

To

My Parents

If management is the process of converting information into action, then it is clear that management success depends primarily on what information is chosen and how the conversion is executed. The difference between a good manager and a poor manager lies at this point.

—Jay W. Forrester

Foreword

The purpose of this book is to introduce managers to some of the basic concepts of establishing a management and technical information center and to describe methods of improving, expanding, and evaluating existing information centers. Teachers and students of business management will find this book helpful as a practical text in the interrelated fields of management and information. It presupposes no prerequisite courses, but does assume an appreciation of the free enterprise system and the profit motive.

The book departs from the usual approach to information centers in that it does not separate the management information center and the technical information center into separate entities. Technical decisions with no consideration given to overall management plans and policies and management problem solving with little knowledge of technical feasibility are the follies that precede the disaster of business failures. The interdisciplinary requirements of business management can no longer tolerate a schism of information; all the facts are needed to operate a successful business.

I have resisted making this a how-to-do-it book. The businessman in search of such material will find in the bibliography a sampling of the excellent books of that nature that are available. More important, managers should hire professional information specialists and special librarians to implement and operate the type of information center needed by their companies. Just as the act of removing a splinter from a hand does not make a person a surgeon, so reading a how-to-do-it book on the operation of an information center does not substitute for years of professional training and experience.

5

Thus, I have written this as a *what-to-do* book. It calls to the attention of management the information problem the American businessman faces today, and it offers him alternative solutions. In the hope of helping managers assess the information operation from a business point of view, I have attempted to remove the verbal veils with which some centers enshroud their activities. Rather than astound the practical reader with descriptions of equipment of the future which is as yet impractical for his needs, I have tried to indicate realistically some of the trends toward national and international information networks which his company may be able to join. Wherever possible, I have listed reliable sources of information that are currently available to the managers and directors of companies in the hope they will benefit from this added knowledge.

My hope is that this book will alert the practical businessman to the critical importance of information to management action and will show him some ways of coping with the information problems he faces.

MORTON F. MELTZER

Acknowledgments

The effort that goes into writing a book on information must by its very nature depend on all those who in the author's lifetime have revealed to him various information sources and information processing techniques. A fact gathered here, an item learned there, a study made in one place, a successful undertaking accomplished in another area, all contribute to a man's knowledge when he works with information.

However, the more immediate assistance given the author in preparing this book rightfully deserves acknowledgment. The publishing companies that granted me permission to quote from their copyrighted works were generous. The Martin Marietta Corporation, Orlando division, has been cooperative in offering me an opportunity to manage its information center and to continue to "learn by doing." The information center staff which I direct has offered welcome encouragement during the writing of this book, and I particularly want to thank Mrs. Mona C. Griffith, chief librarian, and Richard M. Mellon, literature research analyst, who read the manuscript and offered constructive suggestions. Mrs. Ann Mann's professional editorial talents and dynamic enthusiasm contributed to the readability of this book. Joseph Field's artwork was undertaken with a spirit of understanding that is manifest in the finished illustrations. Arthur Koski's editorial advice and suggestions aided in making the book encompass all businesses and industries and thus be applicable to the entire field of business management. Mrs. Betty L. Holmes's typing and retyping of the original manuscript is deeply appreciated and reflects her perseverance and understanding. But, in the final analysis, the author assumes full responsibility for what is included here and hopes it reflects well on all those who contributed constructively to its publication.

Contents

> Information, including management infor-
> mation, is growing by the microsecond and
> even the nanosecond. We cannot turn off
> the flow. We had therefore better learn to
> control it—and we are already running late.
> —HOWELL M. ESTES

I

The Proliferation of Information

The management and technical information centers of American
industry are belatedly being revealed as major corporate assets.
Businessmen and managers, engineers and scientists, executives and
administrators are being made aware that the information center
is not simply an overhead service costing so many thousand dollars
each year but is, rather, a vital force in the company. No longer
considered merely a musty storehouse of information, the information center has become a dynamic dispenser of facts. It not only
pays its own way; it is part of the profit-making team, preventing duplication of effort through efficient retrieval and dissemination of
data.

Information centers are essential to industry. In attempting to increase business and recruit top personnel, farsighted management
emphasizes equally management and technical information centers,
laboratories, personnel, plant facilities, and proximity to institutions
of higher learning.

The flood of management and technical information pouring from
government and military sources, colleges and university centers, industrial and scientific laboratories makes it almost impossible for
professional people to keep up with the state of the art in their own

Note: Sources of the quotations that appear at the beginning of each chapter are
    listed under "Notes" at the back of the book. Footnotes are listed following
    these citations.

specialties, let alone in related fields. Information centers can and do resolve this problem. Information specialists scan the current publications and journals, select those articles of interest and importance to their clients, abstract the information, and inform appropriate individuals of the material. Selective dissemination of information permits scientists and managers to pursue their professions while keeping informed of current events in their specialties and saving countless man-hours of valuable time.

Information centers also save their companies millions of dollars simply by preventing duplication of research. A search of the current literature prior to the start of a research project can avoid wasting time and money. "In 1950 an article on the application of Boolean algebra to electrical circuits appeared in a Soviet Academy of Science journal. Though an English abstract was later published in *Mathematical Reviews,* it was not 'discovered' until five years later—after several teams of mathematicians in several U.S. companies had spent more than 15 man-years in unsuccessful attempts to solve the problem." [1] A trip to the company information center, if the company had one, could have saved all this wasted time, money, and talent.

Not only does the information center deal with facts from the past (as in the preparation of bibliographies) and with present occurrences (as in the maintenance of a current awareness program), but it also helps management plan for the future by providing information on new markets, product needs, and industry trends.

Any company whose management plans for it to grow and be profitable requires pertinent, timely information. It must also be accurate, relevant, and reasonable in cost. The well-planned and well-administered information center fulfills these needs and thus should be viewed as an asset on the company's balance sheet.

THE INFORMATION PROBLEM

Let us look at the so-called information explosion in one area: science and technology. Between 35,000 and 50,000 technical periodicals are published annually throughout the world—in fact, the number may be closer to 100,000. These journals contain nearly two million technical articles within their covers. And this quantity of scientific papers is increasing by about 6 percent each year. Exhibit 1 illustrates this proliferation of information.

But the quantity of information is only one part of the problem. Even if one could absorb the mass of technical information printed, separating the wheat from the chaff, the relevant from the irrelevant, the original from the redundant would constitute an information crisis unto itself.

What is more, the time element in publishing information has presented serious problems. There is a lapse of at least six months between the date a scientific paper is submitted to a journal and the date it is published. Thus, in addition to the problems of quantity and quality of information, the question of timeliness arises.

When the perceptive manager views the facts on scientific and technical information against a background of increasing research and development costs, decreasing technical manpower pools, and frequent duplication of efforts within his own organization he soon realizes the necessity for an information center. (And let us keep in mind that we are talking only about the information which appears in the readily available literature of journals and periodicals. When the material in technical reports, oral presentations, specifications, and so on is considered, the problem of information retrieval and dissemination staggers the imagination.)

The management information crisis is just as critical as the problems posed by the scientific and technical data explosion. The increasing volume of information needed on money, manpower, manufacturing, and marketing within an organization is overwhelming. Add to this the available (but not necessarily quickly accessible) data regarding areas of interest outside the company, such as competition and developments within industry, and the quantity assumes major proportions. The need for managers to receive relevant and accurate information in time for them to make meaningful decisions demonstrates the need of every company for a management and technical information center.

The *quality* of information supplied to management is critical. Burying important marketing facts among a mass of statistical data causes the price for low-quality information to skyrocket. If employees in one skill area are released to the open labor market from one segment of the company while another division spends hundreds of thousands of dollars recruiting the same talent, losses are compounded in the most extravagant way. Missed schedules, inventory shortages, and bad investments are typical of the evils produced by poor-quality information.

Then there is the element of *lack* of information. Although no information at all may perhaps be better than poor information, in business the result of ignorance is not bliss but rather a sharp downward trend in the profit curve. Even though the information is available, it may not be accessible; and this frustrating situation plagues top management constantly. One of the most disheartening of all situations is to discover that essential data are accessible—too late to be of value to the problem at hand.

The User

Let us examine the problem from the point of view of the information user. No matter how brilliant the scientist or how astute the manager, there is a limit to the amount of information he can absorb

Exhibit 1. The Information Explosion in Science and Technology

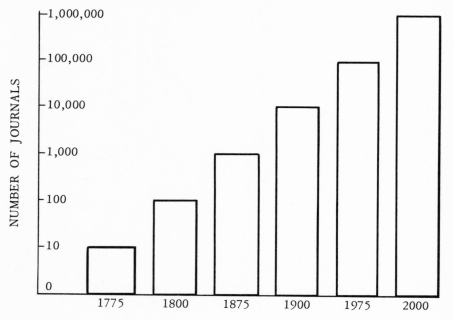

and retain. In addition to the basic store of information he carries in his brain, the user needs temporary access to facts in order to solve problems and make decisions based on the best available data. Much of this material is ephemeral in nature and changes daily. Other facts are needed for reference only or as context within which hard-core information takes on a different meaning for each situation. The administrator or manager cannot, indeed should not, deal with the deluge of detailed items, but they should be available to him when needed.

Too frequently the emphasis has been on the types of information available with little thought given to the various users of the information. Very often the material needed by the scientific community is the same as is required by the managerial group. Similarly, the facts needed by top management in a business are sometimes the same ones needed by first levels of supervision to perform their operations. The engineer who devises a system without regard to cost factors, the personnel manager who hires without consideration for skill mix, the sales director who commits deliveries without knowledge of production time and manufacturing backlog—all are guilty of a parochial approach to their professions. Classifying information in technical or management categories sometimes has the result of limiting the flow of that information. In reality information cuts across all disciplines and should be made available to all potential users within the company. Intelligent forecasting, wise decision making, and practical problem solving require all types of information in varying amounts at every level of management. Narrow attitudes toward information usually show up in narrow profits for the company.

Information is just one of the many tools available to decision makers and problem solvers. It is a means to an end, not an end in itself. Data provided by the information center are of no value unless used by its clients. Getting potential users to request and use the material is as important to an information center as is acquiring the relevant information. Thus, by taking the user into consideration, management is faced with a twofold problem: (1) controlling the proliferation of information and (2) encouraging the exploitation of information by company personnel.

Many companies tend to look at their information problems in a segmented way: to establish a technical information center or a personnel data pool or a planning and control department. What is needed is a total view of the problem—a view from the top. And if top managers feel the problem is too unimportant to deal with, they should heed the words of Francis Bello: "Mankind is learning things so fast that it's a problem how to store information so it can be found when needed. Not finding it costs the U.S. over $1 billion a year." [2] How many dollars is your company contributing to this billion-dollar deficit each year?

Other resources, money or physical equipment, for instance, do not confer any dis-
tinction. What does make a business distinct and what is its peculiar resource is its
ability to use knowledge of all kinds—from
scientific and technical knowledge to social, economic, and managerial knowledge.
It is only in respect to knowledge that a
business can be distinct, can therefore produce something that has a value in the
market place.

—PETER F. DRUCKER

II

The Information Challenge

Frequently the terms "library," "company library," and "special
library" are used to define the purposes of the information
center. The general term "library" is better reserved to describe
the familiar public, school, and college libraries. Such a library provides information for recreational needs, educational purposes, and
cultural enrichment. Its collections include fiction and nonfiction
books, magazines, newspapers, journals, slides, films, records, maps,
and framed reproductions of art masterpieces.

The library's material is organized so that its clients can readily
make use of the collection. It usually offers a reader's advisory service, a reference section, and a limited information service. The public library also aids adults who are educating themselves as well as individuals enrolled in formal study programs. It generally supports
community civic and cultural groups.

Exhibit 2. FUNCTIONS OF AN INFORMATION CENTER

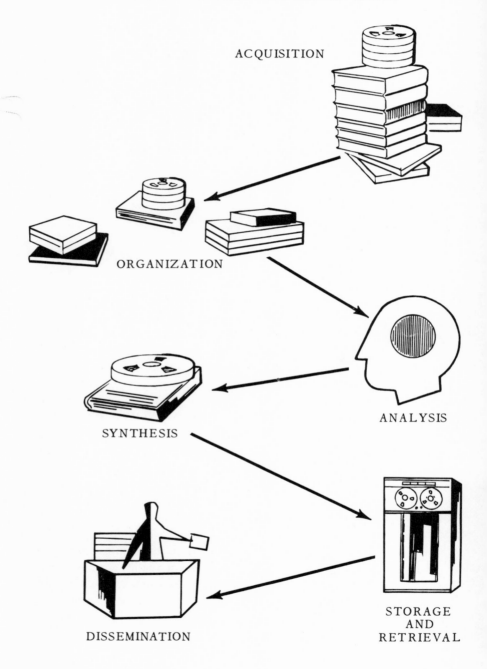

ACQUISITION

ORGANIZATION

ANALYSIS

SYNTHESIS

STORAGE
AND
RETRIEVAL

DISSEMINATION

THE SPECIAL LIBRARY

In contrast to the functions of a library, a management and technical information center performs the following functions:
- Acquires information needed by the company.
- Organizes the material for later retrieval.
- Analyzes the documents for value, validity, and completeness.
- Synthesizes the information to give it broader meaning, greater application, and a point of reference.
- Stores the data for ready reference.
- Disseminates the information to those who need it.

Exhibit 2 illustrates these basic activities.

The Special Libraries Association describes the objectives of the company or special library in these words: "The special library acquires, organizes, maintains, utilizes, and disseminates the information materials germane to the organization's activities." [3] The special library is the main source of information in areas related to the objectives and missions of the company of which it is a part. Its staff selects and acquires data for the present and future needs of the business and presents this material to its clients before they request it or in response to direct queries. To fulfill requests from clients, special library personnel often call on the resources of other institutions.

In addition to these basic functions, company library researchers conduct literature searches and compile the data in bibliographies and reports. Staff members index and abstract technical reports, journals, and periodicals; prepare a current awareness program; provide translation services; and publish lists of the latest acquisitions. Usually the special library's collection consists of reports and periodicals which cover thoroughly a specific field of knowledge; or else it is mission-oriented and crosses the lines of several disciplines. The material making up its resources may also include audiovisual items, preprints, theses and dissertations, specifications, patents, catalogs, and maps.

The information center, then, is the special library with the added function of analyzing and synthesizing the information needed by management, staff, and the technical personnel of the organization. It does not replace the company library, but rather expands its services and becomes the major source and disseminator of information for immediate and practical purposes. In reviewing, evaluating, and integrating the documents that are acquired, cataloged, and indexed, the information center emphasizes the content of the material rather than the material itself. Instead of reacting to requests for specific information, the center librarian more often acts to fulfill anticipated information needs of the company.

THE CHALLENGE TO MANAGEMENT

From a management standpoint, the information center provides a nucleus for the collection of management and technical information; acts as a clearinghouse for the information needed by management for decision making, planning, and control; and offers information for management development.

Most companies subscribe to various journals and buy books relating to their fields of interest, whether or not the organization has a formal library or information center to act as a central source for the collection of information. But before these documents can be exploited to the maximum benefit of the company they must be organized. Duplicate subscriptions to magazines, multiple purchases of the same books, and documents that cannot be located when needed are only a few of the costly symptoms of the need for an information center. No matter how much material a company may accumulate, if it cannot quickly be brought to the attention of appropriate individuals, or if it is not easily accessible to those who need it, valuable time and money are being squandered. Long-distance telephone calls and trips to track down information which is readily available in the organization are needlessly wasteful ways to conduct a business.

Making decisions, formulating plans, and exerting controls are among the most important functions of management. When decisions must be postponed because needed information is lacking, the immediate and urgent requirement for an information center is obvious. When analysis of bad decisions reveals they were made without considering available facts which were either not organized or not conveniently located and not known to be available, the vital importance of the information center is brought into the spotlight.

Most managers have readily at hand business data and financial reports compiled by their marketing and financial divisions, and they make their decisions accordingly. But the technical data which must be fed into the decision-making mechanism are usually not available in a ready-to-comprehend format. This function the efficient information center can perform.

The center can provide top management with summaries and abstracts of important technical data bearing on management decisions. If more complete detail is needed, the document itself can be withdrawn from the files for closer inspection by the decision makers. Also, if the information center is routinely informed of proposed new developments that could affect objectives and other areas under consideration, it will be in a position to supply relevant information in quantity.

Such facts as how the company has handled a similar problem in the past, how competing organizations have dealt with a question, additional items that should be taken under advisement before a complete evaluation of a problem is made, forecasts by experts that might influence decisions—all can be made available through the information center. The center does not perform the decision-making function, but certainly it can provide the information to make decisions more meaningful. And there is another side to the coin. Just as the information center has a responsibility to keep management informed, management has an equal obligation to keep the center informed of new fields in which it is interested and of changes being considered within the current areas of activity.

Management is a dynamic profession, regardless of the business in which it functions, and as such it must develop and grow or it will act as a drain on the company's profits. A static management does not merely become stagnant; it actually causes the organization to lose the prominence it already has attained in its field. The information center can and should provide top-level managers with summaries of current management thinking as revealed in journals, books, symposium proceedings, and technical articles. In conjunction with a formal management development program, it can provide useful bibliographies and recommended reading lists to middle managers. The first-line supervisor can be exposed to the principles, skills, and tools of management through textbooks and papers on business and management supplied by the information center.

THE CHALLENGE TO TECHNICAL PERSONNEL

In addition to the important contributions made by the information center to management, it can also provide similar services to the technical staff. It can help engineers and scientists to survive the aptly named information explosion. According to the *Wilson Library Bulletin,* "The well-recognized exponential curve of growth in the number of scientists and in the amount of scientific literature published since the seventeenth century has produced in 1965 more than one million papers, with every indication that this number will double again by 1980." [4] The information center can convert this explosion of information into mental energy useful to the company's technical staff. Properly controlled, this vast amount of information can avert duplication of research and waste of time and money.

Before any scientific or technical task is started, the information center should be requested to make a search of the literature on the subject. A retrospective search may reveal that the task has already been accomplished and that results are available.

> A major electronics firm recently paid $8 million for two patented inventions only to find that it had wasted its money. The two patents had no value: buried in the Patent Office files were patents showing that both ideas had been anticipated by earlier inventors. Such failures in information retrieval occur, even though the Patent Office has one of the world's best-indexed files and 1,000 skilled patent examiners. [5]

The information center's search through indexes and abstract journals (*Engineering Index, Chemical Abstracts,* and so on) will alert scientists and engineers to what has already been done on a particular problem and what is yet to be accomplished. To cover the lag between the date an item is published and the date it appears in an indexing or abstracting service, the center's subject specialists should constantly scan the current literature and select those articles pertinent to the company's present and planned activities. These articles should be analyzed, synthesized, abstracted, and cataloged for current dissemination and later retrieval.

The functioning information center not only acts to prevent duplication of effort and save the time and talent of management and technical personnel, but it also acts as a catalyst for creativity. Few companies can afford the serendipity approach to discovery. On the other hand, cross-fertilization of seemingly unrelated ideas that appear in a bibliography may well result in the scientific break-through of tomorrow. The wheel should not have to be reinvented every time an experiment is begun. By reminding its patrons of what has transpired in the past and alerting them to what is currently being done in a particular field, the center may spark the idea that adds profits to a company's coffers.

CATEGORIES OF MANAGEMENT INFORMATION

Too frequently the information center in industry has been re-stricted to functioning only as a technical information center. Its ma-terial is intended mainly for scientific and technical groups; and although it may be open to management and administration, it is generally usable only by research and development departments.

To provide a meaningful service the information center must sat-isfy the needs of many kinds of users. The material it contains should apply to all segments of the company and be readily accessible to all clients. As the company grows and its operations become more com-plex, its needs for multidiscipline information increase correspond-ingly. Although the presence of a highly efficient information system is no guarantee that the enterprise will be profitable, the absence of an adequate collection of information may seriously hamper a com-pany's effectiveness.

The following categories include the material necessary for the efficient operation of a well-run management and technical informa-tion center: manpower information, monetary information, material information, and marketing information.

Manpower information covers personnel. Individual personnel records containing confidential matter such as current performance appraisals, job histories, pay rates, and employee potential should re-main within the confines of the personnel department. But a summa-tion of an analytical and synthesized report on the personnel files should be available to management through the center. The basic manpower data mandatory for intelligent decision making are skill profiles of present employees, manpower requirements for current and future work, rate of attrition by skills, labor relations precedents file, and annual attendance records by work area.

Monetary information stored in the center, like manpower data, should be in summary form. The finance department, directed by the controller, should of course maintain the various accounts of the general ledger and perform the customary financial functions inherent in good accounting and business practices. But broad-based financial reports should be available in the information center and updated periodically according to the nature and changes of the reports—cash flow, operating ratios, profit and loss statements, balance sheets, and planned versus actual budgets.

Material information covers the complete spectrum of facts regarding planning, scheduling, production, and distribution as well as research, development, and engineering. Although status information about individual activities is maintained in each of these areas, the relationships of all of them are so intricately interdependent that management should approach them from a Gestalt point of view rather than an atomistic piecemeal evaluation. For example, much long-range strategic planning depends on the results from the research and development groups. Schedules are meaningless unless they are linked to realistic inventory controls, production figures, and shipping information. Tactical short-range plans will remain only theoretical unless consideration is given to manufacturing and engineering activities. From all these fragments of information, top management must assemble an overall picture of the company's status. The information center should receive broad coverage reports from operational areas and summarize the data in meaningful reports and charts for assimilation by company executives.

Marketing information includes internally generated sales data and near-term marketing campaign material as well as such important externally originated facts as the political, social, and economic aspects of the affected market areas. Marketing trends, buying habits, and new international, national, and state regulatory requirements are examples of the material needed by marketing personnel. Like the other major sources of information, this material should be analyzed, synthesized, and arranged in a format suited to the needs of the users. Typical of the summarized marketing data that should be available through the information center and considered by decision-making elements of the company are details on competitive products and companies, results of applicable consumer studies, pricing information, sales promotion plans and techniques, and development of new markets and products.

CATEGORIES OF USERS

Just as information has been described as falling into four major categories, so may the patrons of the management and technical information center be viewed as members of four distinct groups: top management, middle management, first-level supervision, and operating personnel.

Top managers need highly distilled, meaningful information cutting across organizational lines. To the executive suite all information flows, and from it broad administrative policies are issued. The men and women who make up this group are accountable for the success or failure of a company. Strategic long-range planning regarding mergers, acquisitions, capital, new facilities, and new product lines are the concern of these executive managers. They are interested not in details—only in the big picture. Upon their decisions rests the fate of the company. They must have accurate, reliable information that is pertinent and timely. The information center fulfills this need with its synthesized and summarized information gathered from internal and external sources.

Middle managers solve the problems and make the decisions required to fulfill the goals and policies established by top management. Here again the information center can provide the material upon which these men act. An article describing how the company successfully or unsuccessfully handled a similar situation in the past provides guidelines for current undertakings. Knowing what other companies did in like circumstances aids these men in their work. Naturally, people in middle management require more detailed information than do those in top management, and they depend a great deal on their subordinates to supply them with data for final decisions.

First-line supervisors are responsible for making sure the product or service is produced on time within cost and at the quality level set by the company. These men must be kept informed of what is happening in their fields, so that they may apply the latest methods and

Exhibit 3. LEVELS OF INFORMATION AND MANAGEMENT

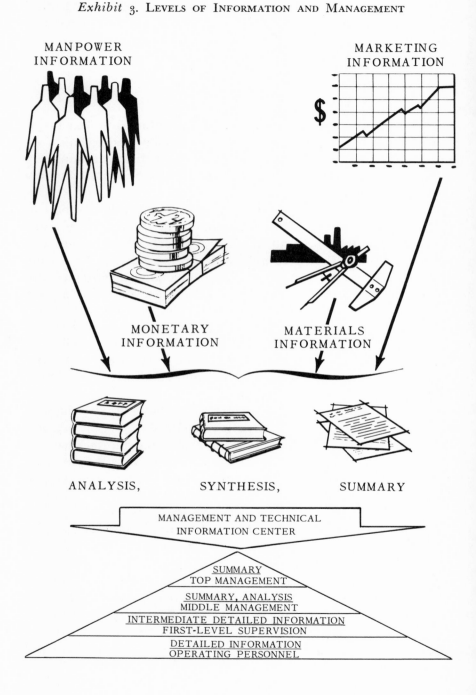

techniques to their jobs. Those who are assigned to areas of research and development constantly use the information center for bibliographic services and retrospective searches to aid them in solving their problems. Besides depending on the center as a most important source of much-needed data, they supply it with the bulk of the in-house reports and documents published by the company.

In too many cases the operating personnel use the management and technical information center only infrequently. This is their own and the company's loss. Obviously the information center is not a recreational library, but it should offer material valuable to rank-and-file employees who are anxious to improve themselves. Collateral reading matter from company courses should be available, and so should the textbooks used in conjunction with formal adult educational programs offered in the area.

Exhibit 3 illustrates the methods by which the management and technical information center disseminates the pertinent information to the appropriate users in the right format at the right time.

But we must be on guard to prevent
duplication—eliminate obsolete items—and
avoid unnecessary details. Too much reporting puts a heavy burden on citizens,
industry in general, and particularly on
small business. . . . Our objective is simply
this: (1) to simplify reports, (2) to discon-
tinue reports where possible, (3) to save
the time of the individual businessman as
well as industry in general. . . . This
should result in a long-term saving of time
and money by the Government, business,
and the general public.

—LYNDON B. JOHNSON

III

Closing the Information Gap

After acknowledging the need for a continuous flow of information, management must take steps to insure that the flow is
smooth, uninterrupted, and relevant. The first move is to examine
old problems which may cause interruptions in the stream of information. The problems of information flow in any organization break
down into three major areas: the source of the information, the information itself, and the recipient of the information.

Corollary considerations that must be taken into account when
management looks at its information structure are the method of
transmitting the information, its purpose, and its desired or probable
effect.

Exhibit 4 is a flow model depicting these six elements of information.

When he was a senator, Vice President Hubert H. Humphrey incisively stated the problem: "Are management and operating personnel . . . getting the information which they need and want, when they want it, in the way that they want it?" [6]

Sources of information. Information comes from internal or external sources or from a combination of the two. Typical of internally generated data are profit and loss statements, personnel records, wage and salary rates, and facilities lists. External information covers such areas as economic, political, and social data as well as scientific and technical information from other companies, academic institutions, trade associations, and the Federal Government. The most meaningful information is derived from a combination of external and internal sources. For example, inventory control data must include such facts as stock on hand (internal), orders to be delivered (external and internal—that is, the order comes from an external source, but the information about it is generated internally), materials produced within the company (internal), materials provided by suppliers and subcontractors (external). Schedules are based on manpower and materials available to do the job (internal), but are influenced by contractual dates that must be met (external). Plans for new product lines depend on marketing data (external), but are constrained by the company's know-how and resources (internal).

The information itself may be in the form of a statement of fact or raw data, evaluations, or summaries. This spectrum of information nearly parallels the receipt of information from operating personnel and first-line supervision through middle management to top management. Raw data or factual statements may range from an itemized listing of accounts payable to highly specialized scientific and technical formulas. The worth of evaluated material varies in importance to various levels of users. This material may be linked with related information to give it greater meaning. The summarized information is a distillation of the collected data for broad policy decision making and problem solving.

Methods of transmitting data. Whether information is transmitted orally or in writing is determined by the information source, the information itself, and the person requesting the information. A scientist requiring data from a fellow scientist working for the same company will frequently obtain the needed information by asking for it. If distance prohibits face-to-face conversation, he makes his request

Exhibit 4. Information Flow Model

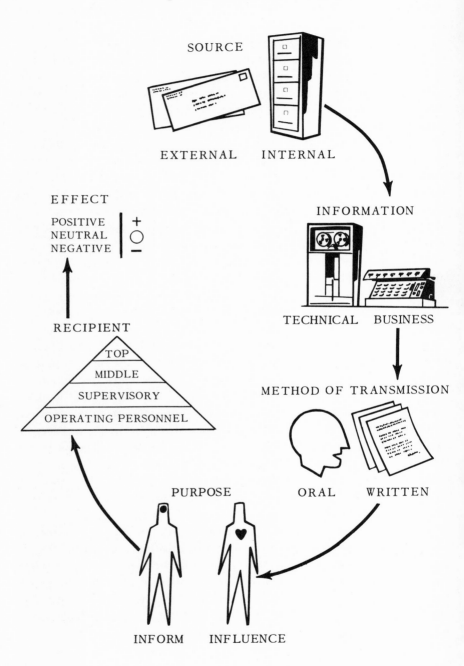

by telephone. This person-to-person transmission is taken a step further when a meeting or colloquium is held on a specific topic. Information is transferred from the speaker to the audience during the talk, then from the audience to the speaker in a question-and-answer period. One advantage of such oral communication is that any vague points can be clarified on the spot.

The most frequently used medium for transferring information is the written word. It has the advantage of being available for later reference, if desired, and it can reach more people in less time than can person-to-person dialogue. It also has the mixed blessing of appearing authoritative and final. And it has one distinct disadvantage —you can't ask it questions to clarify ambiguous passages. The printed word usually appears in most businesses in the form of management and scientific reports. In addition, internal oral presentations are often followed by publication of a paper, which may vary somewhat from what was actually spoken. Later, from external sources comes printed information in journals and trade publications. And, later still, the material appears in secondary publications as abstracts and indexes. Other methods of processing data range from microfilm and magnetic tape to punched cards and closed circuit television.

Purposes of information. Although there are many reasons for presenting information, the major single purpose is simply to transmit facts upon which meaningful decisions can be made. Too often phrased in business jargon or technical terminology, such material sometimes appears designed to confuse rather than enlighten. Too, the method of presenting information can influence the reader as much as the information itself does. Sometimes what is not included in a report could throw an entirely different light on a subject. Also, there is the publication whose main purpose is personal publicity: It has no significant information value, consumes the time of managers, incurs unnecessary processing and storage costs, and clogs the information channels with drivel.

The effect of information is the feedback element in this information flow. The purpose of a communication may be one thing, but the effect is often something entirely different. The purpose of the Surgeon General's report on cigarette smoking was to warn of the possible dangers of smoking. But the effects of the statement on the tobacco industry were the development of new marketing techniques, diversification of product lines, and additional funding for research projects.

The Information Gap

Having briefly looked at the information flow, we can now proceed to establish the parameters that determine the information gap $(\triangle I)$. In a very basic formula, the information gap (Exhibit 5) is the difference between the information needed (I_n) and the informa-

Exhibit 5. INFORMATION GAP

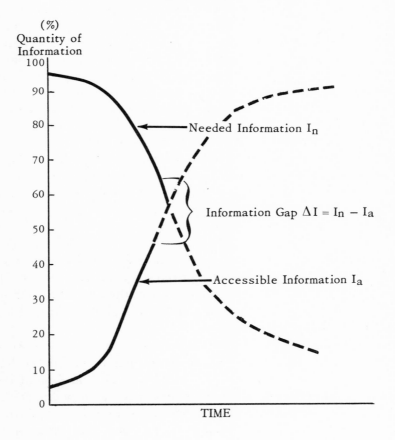

tion accessible (I_a) to make a decision, solve a problem, or continue or cease an activity. Thus:

$$\triangle I = I_n - I_a$$

Accessible information is the data that can be obtained from the storehouse of available information. Information depositories range from facts stored in the mind and in personal libraries, to the information centers inside and outside a company facility, to academic and national library systems. It is worth noting that, because of time limitations or because of safeguards placed on the data, available information may not be accessible. For example, each year the design data on new automobiles are available many months before the cars appear in showrooms, but the information is accessible to only a few people. The plans for building a hydrogen bomb are available; they are accessible (it is hoped) to a tightly restricted group of people in our country.

Depending on the subject under consideration, the types of information needed to make decisions may run the gamut from accounting data to zymurgy formulas (a branch of applied chemistry that deals with fermentation processes). Thus the first step of the acquisition phase is developing the negative information—that is, data that will not actually be used in solving the problem, but that determine what material must be made accessible before a decision can be reached. The positive information aspect of the acquisition phase then begins. All data related to the problem at hand are assembled from whatever resources are available. This quantification step is followed by the evaluation phase. And here the emphasis shifts to quality. The information that is germane to the problem at hand is retained; the irrelevant material is returned to storage. This phase takes considerably more time than does the acquisition phase. Analysis, synthesis, and further evaluation are conducted with the information that is retained. But it is also possible that from the accessible information not enough data are available to make an intelligent decision. Breakthroughs in science and new discoveries may be necessary to solve the problem, and, of course, these add to the time needed to reach a go, no-go point.

Two major constraints in closing the information gap are the degree of risk and the time element. The degree of risk (probability of error) is the chance the decision maker is willing to take in making a decision and is determined by the importance of the problem under consideration. The degree of risk (R_d) is inversely proportional to the quantity of information (I_q) available:

$$R_d \propto \frac{1}{I_q}$$

As more and more information becomes accessible, the probability of making a bad decision on the basis of these data becomes less and less (Exhibit 6).

The second major constraint is time. A short time span for solving a problem will limit the amount of information available to apply to

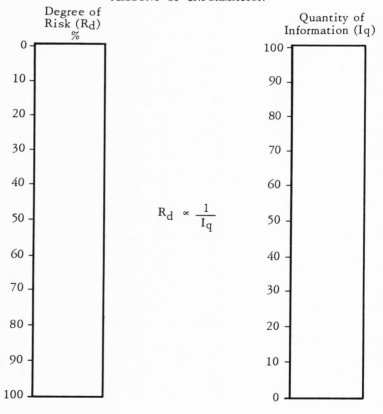

Exhibit 6. CORRELATION OF DEGREE OF RISK TO AMOUNT OF INFORMATION

a solution. The more time one has, the more information he can marshal to his use. As shown in the information gap model (Exhibit 7), the less information one uses in making a decision, the greater the risk of making a bad decision. How wide or how narrow the information gap that can be tolerated in making a decision is influenced by the importance of the decision. Committing the company to a multimillion-dollar effort requires a low degree of risk and a high degree of information; in such a situation, the information gap would close when nearly 90 percent of the information becomes available. By the same token, a decision on whether to hire a file clerk could be made safely when only 30 percent of the factors affect-

Exhibit 7. INFORMATION GAP MODEL

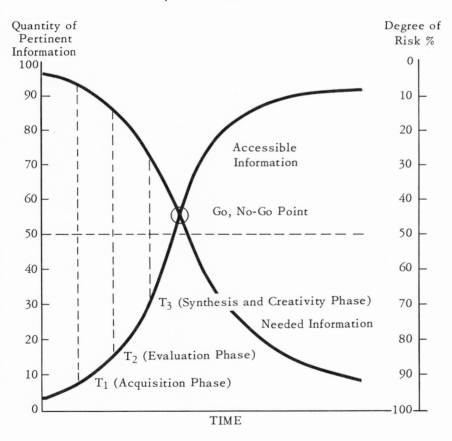

Exhibit 8. INFORMATION SEARCH CYCLE

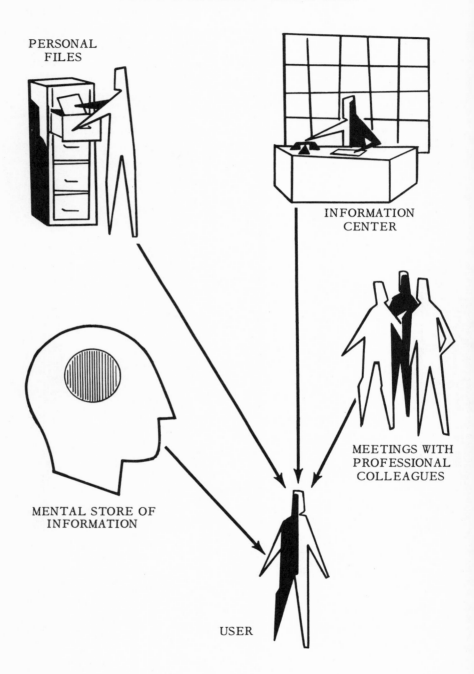

PERSONAL
FILES

INFORMATION
CENTER

MEETINGS WITH
PROFESSIONAL
COLLEAGUES

MENTAL STORE OF
INFORMATION

USER

ing the decision have been brought to the manager's attention; a wide information gap and a high degree of risk could be tolerated in this situation. As the amount of available information becomes accessible, the amount still needed for a meaningful decision decreases. When management determines that enough information has been supplied to make a decision, the information gap is closed.

It should be noted in Exhibit 7 that curves for both information needed and information accessible extend beyond the go, no-go point. That portion of the information-needed curve past the decision point represents the additional information that would be helpful to have, were there no constraints on time and money. In a sense, it is a view of the law of diminishing returns.

In any problem-solving or decision-making function, a certain amount of information is evolved that was neither accessible nor available prior to the start of the project and is not necessarily applicable to the problem at hand. This spin-off of information is described by the curve of accessible information past the go, no-go point. Included in the portion of the needed information curve that appears after the go, no-go point is material that was pertinent to arriving at a decision, but became accessible only after the time limit expired.

ROLE OF THE INFORMATION CENTER

The information center plays a vital role in closing the information gap. By providing an acquisition and dissemination point, it allows the user more time to develop new information and utilize what is already accessible. The user must be taught to include the center in his search cycle, along with the recall of learned data stored in his mind, the information gleaned from discussions with his colleagues, and reference to his personal files and collections (Exhibit 8).

The manager or professional practitioner seeking information will naturally follow the simplest course in securing it. The information which is easiest of access is that stored in his own mind; it will be used first. The next most convenient way to find out what he wants to know is to call upon colleagues. He may then search through his personal files for data applicable to the problem under consideration.

Perhaps his next step will be to waste much valuable time in searching for data which may be available in condensed form in the information center. The center provides the greatest access to information for immediate use as well as for long-term requirements. The user must be taught that the time spent in trying to remember, in talking with associates, and in hunting through files might be put to better use if he were first to find out if the center has what he needs. Rather than allow location to play the decisive role in determining the method of retrieving information, the use of the center should be stressed as the practical professional approach toward decision making.

However, the information center staff must establish user confidence by supplying quality services that meet the patron's needs and that supplement, even in some instances supplant, his former methods of acquiring data. The old merchandising maxim holds true: The best customer is a satisfied customer.

There are three major ways to get managers and operating personnel in the habit of using the center in their efforts to close the information gap:

1. Keep clients and potential clients informed of the services available.
2. Show people how to use these services.
3. Obtain top management backing.

Once it is determined what services the center will provide to its various users, these functions should be publicized by brochures, bulletins, oral presentations, and notices. As services are added or changed, these should be advertised throughout the company. The professional role of the center should be brought to the attention of all.

Once the scope of the center's services is made known, the next procedure is to inform clients how to use these services to the best advantage. Explaining how to ask for information to expedite its retrieval and to guarantee its value is mandatory. Clients must be shown how to use catalogs, indexes, abstract reports, and similar information center tools. Many clients will avail themselves of the center's services only if they themselves can conduct their own bibliographic searches, browse through journals and documents, and read books and reports. A training or orientation program is needed to help these people do this efficiently. By the same token, clients who want the center to provide them with the finished search, reports, data, or information should be informed of the best method of making their wants known to the center's staff.

With top management approval of the information center evidenced both by word and by action, the level of confidence of its patrons will increase and it will be established as a major source for closing the information gap. Just as an organization invests money in laboratories for scientists and engineers to produce information, so must the center be supported as a major company facility to produce information needed by management and operating personnel.

The center acts as a catalyst in closing the information gap. It is an agency whose function is to provide the right information to the man who needs it—on time and in usable form.

The problems of keeping managers informed and providing the up-to-the-minute data needed to make the necessary decisions in all areas of engineering and manufacturing are as complex as the aircraft systems we're producing, and unless our managers could rely on a system of acquiring, translating, analyzing, and disseminating such data, they would be deluged with more information than they could handle—unless we did something about it.

We decided to do something about it.

—W. A. PULVER

IV

Systems Approach to Information

I f meaningful guidelines and policies are to be established for the operation of the information center, the systems approach to information must be followed. By this is meant adopting a five-step process in which the manager (1) sets goals or objectives; (2) determines what problems must be solved to achieve these goals; (3) lists the alternatives by which these problems may be solved and the goals may thus be achieved; (4) decides which of the alternatives offers the optimum results; and (5) implements the plan with a feedback system to make necessary adjustments as goals and values change over a period of time.

SETTING THE GOALS

All information centers should aim to achieve five basic goals: (1) acquire information, (2) organize it, (3) analyze and synthesize it,

(4) maintain it, and (5) disseminate it. Regardless of the type of company the information center serves, the people who patronize it, or the types of information handled within it, it is not truly an information center if its supervisors do not aspire to and attain these goals.

The *acquisition of information* must be a well-planned procedure. A slipshod approach to acquiring information yields slipshod information. A constant awareness of the company's areas of interest by members of the center will indicate the types of information that will be of significant value. The staff of the center cannot afford to overlook any possible source of material. In addition to the conventional sources (books, periodicals, journals, and reports), vital material may appear in such documents as memos, engineering notebooks, tape recordings, trip reports, photos, patents, and maps. External sources of information often prove as valuable as the home-grown variety: financial statements of competitors; industry trends; Department of Commerce statistics; labor news; scientific and technical abstract services; and pending legislation.

The *organization of information* must be along functional lines consistent with the company's needs. Every item must be classified, indexed, abstracted, cataloged, and filed for later retrieval. Whether the system is computerized, mechanized, or manual, the requirements remain the same—only the methods change.

Regardless of the classification system used, it should be adaptable to allow for modifications reflecting the company's developing interests and it should be user-oriented to permit a self-service search for information. In an open-shelf area, most people could find a book on management, such as J. D. Batten's *Tough-Minded Management,* filed under 658 of the familiar Dewey decimal system. But how many could decipher HD38.B33 as the Library of Congress notation for the same material, if they did not know this classification method?

Like the other sections of the firm, the information center's collection must be organized for action. The mission of the center is to provide accurate information on time at the lowest possible cost; the classification scheme that best fulfills this mission is the right one.

Next, the *analysis and synthesis of information.* One of the differences between the special library and the information center is that, in the latter, items of raw data are manipulated into information. The manipulation can be accomplished through analysis or synthesis of the new facts or by applying a combination of these techniques to the original data. Manipulation is the process of putting facts into perspective for meaningful evaluation and use.

When the widely publicized apple fell from a branch onto young Isaac Newton's skull, the event was a fact. The analysis of what caused the apple to fall, the rate of its fall, and so on, combined with the synthesis of these data with similar events, produced the information from which the law of gravity was formulated. It is doubtful that the management of any company would hold its information center responsible for developing basic laws of physics or management science (comparable to the law of gravity) because of this example. But every company management should expect and, indeed, should demand that the information provided it is placed in a meaningful frame of reference.

Along with the manipulation of data should be included the service of providing related or peripheral information. The client should not be burdened with excessive quantities of information, some of which may be of poor quality or hold little relationship to the original request. But when someone asks for the latest information available on the method of maintaining a certain temperature in a given environment, he should be informed that such information is also being investigated by another individual in the company or by a group of people or laboratories outside the company if such is the case. Also, manipulation of data may encompass manipulation of the original question after the inquiry is discussed with the client. Perhaps, in our theoretical inquiry, what the person really wanted was a substance that could withstand or maintain various temperatures in a certain environment.

The information center staff should not be expected to solve problems or to make decisions for managers; its personnel should not be expected to conduct experiments and tests for the company's scientists and engineers. But it is obliged to provide meaningful information to its managerial and technical users so that they can accomplish their tasks more efficiently and more profitably.

The maintenance of information takes into consideration both the physical and the temporal aspects of data. Reports that have been dog-eared and "enhanced" with interlinear and marginal notations usually are of marginal use to the reader. These must be replaced with readable copies. Rolls of microfilm that have been scratched through improper handling or excessive use must be reshot. Aperture cards that have been folded, stapled, spindled, or otherwise mutilated must be prepared again.

In addition to keeping the information in usable condition, the information center staff must see that it is kept current. Revisions to basic documents have to be incorporated—issuing the revisions apart from the original document can be foolhardy and dangerous—and the client has to be informed that changes have occurred. The information center has the responsibility to inform the client when documents have been superseded by other reports.

Basic reference books must be kept up to date. With new nations coming into being almost as a matter of routine, the atlas purchased in December is out of date by the middle of January. Dictionaries of technical terms become obsolete before the ink dries on their pages. Scientists working in the frontiers of the unknown coin new words and symbols to communicate their breakthroughs. The worthwhile information center must keep up with these events; it must maintain the latest reference books and reports for its management and technical clients.

The information center that does not provide for *dissemination of its material* is a warehouse—a glorified storage room. How often the man looking for information goes to the center only to be told: "Sorry, that information has been placed on limited distribution and your name is not on the list." "We have information on microfilm, but we have no viewer." "Here's the information you asked for, but I'm afraid we don't have the revisions to it." Or: "All we have left is our own reference copy, and we can't let anyone borrow that." Subtle are the ways of denying access to information.

The information center that boasts of its neatly arranged stacks and nothing else is a candidate for the next overhead cut. The center is to be used, not viewed. It must provide information, not just store it. When a client does not receive the material he needs he has two alternatives. He can continue his work without benefit of the needed data (and ignorance is not bliss—not when it is costly to a company). Or he can develop the information on his own initiative and run the risk of duplicating what has already been done—a waste of time, talent, and dollars.

Determining the Problems

To fulfill the goals of acquiring, organizing, manipulating, maintaining, and disseminating information, several problems must be recognized and resolved by the administrator of the information group: Who will be served? What types of information will be handled? When will the information be provided? Where will dissemination take place? Why will the center offer its services? How will the center accomplish its goals?

Who will be served? As a profitable firm knows its customers and their needs, the staff of an information center must also know who its clients are and what information they need. Will only top management benefit from the activities of the center? Can middle management avail itself of the material collected? May first levels of supervision be permitted access to the files? Will all employees from the president to the janitor use the facilities?

What types of information? Rather than determining the clients vertically according to organizational hierarchy, a better method may be to define the center horizontally by disciplines. Perhaps only technical and scientific information will be handled, or only financial data. The material issued might be restricted solely to facts regarding personnel. Once it is determined what types of information will be provided, on the basis of who will be served, the various levels of patrons will dictate various levels of information. Top managers needing summary reports and trend indications, middle managers wanting more detailed facts to solve short-range problems, the first-line supervisors seeking information bearing on operation and application are three examples.

When will information be provided? The timeliness of the various system outputs must be determined for the different types and levels of users. The engineer who receives an exhaustive, accurate bibliography on a subject the day after his proposal has been submitted to the customer has received a useless document. On the other hand, the president who is preparing a five-year forecast due next quarter and who receives his information within hours of his request is being overserviced—usually to the detriment of users who really need immediate answers. The problem of establishing priorities as to when information will be delivered must be resolved.

Where will information be delivered? The organization of the company usually determines where information will be delivered. If information centers are established according to fields of interest or disciplines, each center may be its own dispensing unit. A single, centralized center in which are combined the activities of all the specialized centers provides a one-stop department store of information for the users. Selective dissemination of information services allows items of interest to be mailed to clients without the necessity for them to come and ask for the data. Automatic distribution of tables of contents and certain periodicals and reports also eliminates the need for a visit to the center by a client.

Why establish an information center? The reason for setting up the information center must be determined before meaningful policies governing its operation can be established. Is its purpose to centralize acquisitions from the various sources of information? Has it been formed primarily to cut down on the administrative costs? Perhaps its main purpose is to aid research and development personnel to conduct searches in order to avoid duplication of experiments. It is important for management to realize that there may be more than one "why" for an information center's existence.

How will the information center achieve its goals? Determining how the center will fulfill its missions and objectives will depend on the budget, personnel, facilities, and equipment allocated to it. The best-laid plans cannot be accomplished without management backing from the standpoint of both profit and motivation. The method of operating the center is directly related to management approval. The information center is a management tool which, if not kept in good repair, will not serve its purpose when needed.

Listing the Alternatives

Acquisitions. The methods of acquiring information are limited only by imagination. External sources such as Federal and state agencies, universities, and other businesses can supply a host of facts ranging from marketing information to details on scientific experiments. Much of this is available free of charge, some can be obtained by paying a nominal handling charge, and some will cost whatever can be charged for it in the marketplace.

Management must decide the type of information it wants the center to acquire. A free bibliography on baroque music is not worth the postage to a firm dealing in glue making. Likewise, a music publisher would find a report describing the latest breakthrough in resins a ludicrous acquisition. Quality and pertinence of information, not quantity, must be the criteria for determining the acquisitions.

Internally generated material such as financial data, management facts, long-range production schedules, and research and development reports are all candidates for the management and technical information center's acquisition lists. However, ephemeral information such as letters of transmittal and memos confirming receipt of goods belongs in departmental files or in a records retention group. Valuable space of the center should not be wasted on this material.

Periodicals, journals, and magazines can be acquired individually through the publishers or all at once through a broker dealing in acquisitions. Secondary sources such as abstracts and indexes can reduce the number of primary source purchases, except on a request-as-needed basis. Reprints sometimes are more expensive than the original journals in which they appeared.

Acquisition alternatives need not be limited by point of origin (internal versus external sources) or by monetary considerations (free versus at cost versus at market price). Users and their needs should be determining factors. After a basic reference library is built up, subsequent acquisitions should reflect the changing needs of clients. Also, the guidelines for acquisitions should include a policy that permits acquiring information in anticipation of needs. A company doing work in areas related to oceanography, for example, would do well to build up a nucleus of information in this fast-developing discipline. Too often the request for information comes at the time the decision has to be made rather than at the first indication that facts will be needed in the new area.

Organization. The alternatives for organizing the information center's holdings may vary from the conventional to the esoteric. Most readers are familiar with the Dewey decimal classification system, still one of the best systems for arranging books on shelves, particularly where the collection covers broad fields of knowledge and is relatively small. The system has a shortcoming—a lack of detailed subdivisions of knowledge. This has been overcome in the universal decimal classification system, which expands and modifies the original Dewey decimal system and allows for extended classification of narrow fields of knowledge. Less familiar to most people is the Library of Congress classification scheme, falling somewhere between the Dewey system and the universal decimal classification scheme in its use of detail. It is particularly good for huge collections like that of the Library of Congress.

The Government's Committee on Scientific and Technical Information (COSATI) has developed a comprehensive classification scheme. Exhibit 9 shows how the areas of knowledge have been divided into 22 major fields, which have been broken down into groups. The system is hospitable to further breakdown into subgroups on the basis of the needs of individual companies.

Not all the information center's acquisitions need be organized by the same system. Bound periodicals may be better arranged alphabetically than numerically. Usually, for quick retrieval, maps are best classified by geographical area. Patents kept according to the U.S. Patent Office classification method are easier to search. Slides and photographs lend themselves to several methods of cataloging. The important thing is that the material be organized efficiently for easy access.

Analysis and synthesis. Some of the reasons for analyzing and synthesizing data are to produce an evaluation of the material; to prepare a brief summary of the contents without expressing an opinion; to acknowledge the existence of the material.

As managers well know, "you can't judge a book by its cover." Neither can you appraise data by reading a title. The analyst must scan the incoming data and select the items that are applicable to the current and possible future needs of clients. In addition, the items should be referenced to related material so that an employee looking for one bit of information may use these new data as points of reference in his search. Constraints must be placed on the amount of analysis and synthesis to be handled. First, the originator of the material must be considered. References to the source document should reflect the author's intent, although notations as to possible new applications should be included. The analyzer must consider the users of the information, relative to the extent and intent of the

Exhibit 9. COSATI Subject Category List

01 Aeronautics

   01 Aerodynamics
   02 Aeronautics
   03 Aircraft
   04 Aircraft flight instrumentation
   05 Air facilities

02 Agriculture

   01 Agricultural chemistry
   02 Agricultural economics
   03 Agricultural engineering
   04 Agronomy and horticulture
   05 Animal husbandry
   06 Forestry

03 Astronomy and Astrophysics

   01 Astronomy
   02 Astrophysics
   03 Celestial mechanics

04 Atmospheric Sciences

   01 Atmospheric physics
   02 Meteorology

05 Behavioral and Social Sciences

   01 Administration and management
   02 Documentation and information technology
   03 Economics
   04 History, law and political science
   05 Human factors engineering
   06 Humanities
   07 Linguistics
   08 Man - machine relations
   09 Personnel selection, training and evaluation
   10 Psychology (*Individual and group behavior*)
   11 Sociology

06 Biological and Medical Sciences

   01 Biochemistry
   02 Bioengineering
   03 Biology
   04 Bionics
   05 Clinical medicine
   06 Environmental biology
   07 Escape, rescue and survival
   08 Food
   09 Hygiene and sanitation
   10 Industrial (*Occupational*) medicine
   11 Life support
   12 Medical and hospital equipment
   13 Microbiology
   14 Personnel selection and maintenance (*Medical*)
   15 Pharmacology
   16 Physiology
   17 Protective equipment
   18 Radiobiology
   19 Stress physiology
   20 Toxicology
   21 Weapons effects

07 Chemistry

   01 Chemical engineering
   02 Inorganic chemistry
   03 Organic chemistry
   04 Physical chemistry
   05 Radio and radiation chemistry

08 Earth Sciences and Oceanography

   01 Biological oceanography
   02 Cartography
   03 Dynamic oceanography
   04 Geochemistry
   05 Geodesy
   06 Geography
   07 Geology and mineralogy
   08 Limnology
   09 Mining engineering
   10 Physical oceanography
   11 Seismology
   12 Snow, ice and permafrost
   13 Soil mechanics
   14 Terrestrial magnetism

09 Electronics and Electrical Engineering

   01 Components
   02 Computers
   03 Electronic and electrical engineering
   04 Information theory
   05 Subsystems
   06 Telemetry

10 Energy Conversion *(Non-propulsive)*

   01 Conversion techniques
   02 Power sources
   03 Energy storage

11 Materials

   01 Adhesives and seals
   02 Ceramics, refractories and glass
   03 Coatings, colorants and finishes
   04 Composite materials
   05 Fibers and textiles
   06 Metallurgy and metallography
   07 Miscellaneous materials
   08 Oils, lubricants, and hydraulic fluids
   09 Plastics
   10 Rubber
   11 Solvents, cleaners and abrasives
   12 Wood and paper products

12 Mathematical Sciences

   01 Mathematics and statistics
   02 Operations research

Exhibit 9 (concluded)

13 Mechanical, Industrial, Civil and Marine Engineering
01 Air conditioning, heating, lighting and ventilating
02 Civil engineering
03 Construction equipment, materials and supplies
04 Containers and packaging
05 Couplings, fittings, fasteners and joints
06 Ground transportation equipment
07 Hydraulic and pneumatic equipment
08 Industrial processes
09 Machinery and tools
10 Marine engineering
10.1 Submarine engineering
11 Pumps, filters, pipes, tubing and valves
12 Safety engineering
13 Structural engineering

14 Methods and Equipment
01 Cost effectiveness
02 Laboratories, test facilities, and test equipment
03 Recording devices
04 Reliability
05 Reprography

15 Military Sciences
01 Antisubmarine warfare
02 Chemical, biological, and radiological warfare
03 Defense
03.1 Antimissile defense
04 Intelligence
05 Logistics
06 Nuclear warfare
07 Operations, strategy, and tactics

16 Missile Technology
01 Missile launching and ground support
02 Missile trajectories
03 Missile warheads and fuzes
04 Missiles
04.1 Air and space launched missiles
04.2 Surface launched missiles
04.3 Underwater launched missiles

17 Navigation, Communications, Detection and Countermeasures
01 Acoustic detection
02 Communications
02.1 Radio communications
03 Direction finding
04 Electromagnetic and acoustic countermeasures
05 Infrared and ultraviolet detection
06 Magnetic detection
07 Navigation and guidance
08 Optical detection
09 Radar detection
10 Seismic detection

18 Nuclear Science and Technology
01 Fusion devices *(Thermonuclear)*
02 Isotopes
03 Nuclear explosions
04 Nuclear instrumentation
05 Nuclear power plants
06 Radiation shielding and protection
07 Radioactive wastes and fission products
08 Radioactivity
09 Reactor engineering and operation
10 Reactor materials
11 Reactor physics
12 Reactors *(Power)*
13 Reactors *(Non-power)*
14 SNAP technology

19 Ordnance
01 Ammunition, explosives and pyrotechnics
02 Bombs
03 Combat vehicles
04 Explosions, ballistics and armor
05 Fire control and bombing systems
06 Guns
07 Rockets
08 Underwater ordnance

20 Physics
01 Acoustics
02 Crystallography
03 Electricity and magnetism
04 Fluid mechanics
05 Masers and lasers
06 Optics
07 Particle accelerators
08 Particle physics
09 Plasma physics
10 Quantum theory
11 Solid mechanics
12 Solid state physics
13 Thermodynamics
14 Wave propagation

21 Propulsion and Fuels
01 Air breathing engines
02 Combustion and ignition
03 Electric propulsion
04 Fuels
05 Jet and gas turbine engines
06 Nuclear propulsion
07 Reciprocating engines
08 Rocket motors and engines
08.1 Liquid propellant motors
08.2 Solid propellant motors
09 Rocket propellants
09.1 Liquid propellants
09.2 Solid propellants

22 Space Technology
01 Astronautics
02 Spacecraft
03 Spacecraft trajectories and reentry
04 Spacecraft launch vehicles and ground support

analysis or synthesis. A marketing analysis by geographical activities may be just the report needed by a regional leader; a synthesis of the total market picture is more likely to be needed by top management for decision making. The axiom that the whole is greater than any of its parts does not necessarily hold true in the area of analysis. Only one section of a report, for example, may contain material applicable to the needs of a company. In such a case, this bit of information sandwiched among pages of unrelated matter is really the total report as far as the company is concerned.

Maintenance. Alternative methods of maintenance fall into categories of physical maintenance, currentness of material, and retrieval. As mentioned earlier, the physical quality of the source material has to be maintained. Repair or replacement of damaged material must be undertaken to insure its continued usefulness. Binding periodicals in hard covers and microfilming pertinent material are other ways of maintaining the availability of original reports.

Keeping material current is a more demanding requirement. Although a professionally staffed information center can generally be depended on to substitute updated pages of manuals and replace old documents with superseding reports, there are other ways of keeping current. Basic reference books must be replaced periodically to reflect the new items uncovered through research and new technologies. Also, a program of weeding out-of-date material from the files must be planned. Wise decisions made on the basis of outmoded information can be as costly and disastrous as are bad decisions premised on the best of the current data.

The information center is responsible for keeping up a steady flow of information on what is happening in the fields of interest of the company. Subscriptions to journals, attendance at seminars, acquisition of proceedings help to build up a bank of information for potential needs and give an indication of the material that is becoming archival and may no longer be usable.

Maintaining information for retrieval sounds deceptively simple, but think how frequently you have looked in vain for a slip of paper you put away carefully so you would be sure to remember where it was when you needed it. Or remember the time your secretary was absent and her substitute couldn't find anything because "who ever heard of filing the Jones Company account under 'munitions' when everybody files them under 'ordnance'?" And how often have you "let your fingers do the walking through the yellow pages" only to find that you would have listed a service or product in a different way altogether?

Whether information is stored in tabbed folders, punched into cards, or transferred onto magnetic tape, it is useless if it cannot be retrieved quickly. One way to maintain these files is to establish a consistent method of cataloging. A thesaurus of terms such as the Engineers Joint Council *Thesaurus* or the one recently devised by the Federal Government under Project Lex will at least permit the exercise of a modicum of control in identifying material. Also, special classification schemes and subject headings oriented to various types of businesses are available through the Special Libraries Association. If football is played to the rules of baseball on a soccer field, the spectators will be unable to follow the game. The same holds true for maintaining information in industry. The person who seeks an output from the information system has to know how the input was made to the system originally or both efforts will be to no avail.

Dissemination. The alternative ways to disseminate information may range from an informal conversation to a high-speed printout from the computer. As the center acquires a store of information, it should be recorded and published in a list or bulletin of the new items. The amount of material acquired will determine the frequency with which this bulletin is published.

Automatic routing of particular journals and magazines to interested clients is another method of dissemination. Selective dissemination of information—whereby a client's needs are profiled and matched against the new acquisitions, and a selective listing is then sent to him—is an even more sophisticated method of dispensing data.

In addition to disseminating information that is readily available in the center, a system should be established so that clients are informed of information which is available in their specific fields and is obtainable from external sources. Abstract services and indexing publications should be scanned for material that is germane to the company's needs, and the appropriate individuals should be informed of the availability of this information.

Exhibit 10. DECISION MATRIX FOR ACQUISITIONS

	Acquires Material Already Existing in Company	Acquires Basic Reference Collection	Acquires Current Books and Journals	Acquires Internal Reports	Acquires External Reports	Acquires Secondary Journals (Abstracts and Indexes)	Acquires Special Holdings (Maps, Slides, Specifications)	Acquires Material in Anticipation of Needs	Establishes Interlibrary Loan System	Establishes Ordering Systems for Books, Journals, and Reports	Establishes Policies for Determining Acquisitions
Cost	8	5	3	8	4	2	1	4	3	6	2
Timeliness of Information	3	4	8	10	9	5	7	10	7	4	8
Ease of Operation	9	7	8	7	5	8	2	4	3	8	9
Training Required	8	6	7	9	7	3	3	1	1	2	3
Speed of Operation	5	4	4	6	5	7	4	5	4	9	8
Aid to User	3	5	8	7	9	10	8	10	9	7	7
TOTALS	36	31	38	47	39	35	25	34	27	36	37

Exhibit 11. DECISION MATRIX FOR ORGANIZATION

	Arrange Books by Subject or Author	Shelf Journals and Periodicals by Title	File Reports Numerically by Sequential Acquisition Number	Record Titles, Authors, and Subjects of All Acquisitions on Cards and File	Adopt an Established Classification System for Arranging Books	Use an Established Subject Heading List for Cataloging Books, Journals, Reports	Obtain Catalog Cards from Library of Congress When Available	Create Own Method of Subject Indexing Acquisitions Peculiar to Your Industry
Cost	8	9	7	3	3	2	8	1
Ease of Operation	10	10	7	2	8	9	9	3
Training Required	9	9	7	1	3	3	5	1
Speed of Operation	8	8	5	3	5	4	6	5
Aid to User	2	7	5	10	9	10	9	10
Reliability	3	7	2	9	9	9	9	9
TOTALS	40	50	33	28	37	37	46	29

In those information centers that handle financial data, scheduling information, and materials flow, certain reports should be distributed daily so that management may undertake corrective action as a result of analyzing the data. However, this information should be so structured as to be exceptional rather than routine. Management by exception is maintained by producing incisive reports that highlight deviations from the norm. Again, the frequency with which the reports are published will depend on the nature of the material. A daily profit and loss statement would be as useless as an annual routing of daily newspapers.

MAKING THE DECISION

Once it is determined that an information center is needed and should be established, it must be decided to what extent the five goals cited earlier will be pursued. A decision matrix for each of the five goals should be presented. Exhibits 10 through 14 are based on the concept of establishing a management and technical information center in a medium-size company. These matrices should be used only as guidelines in preparing decision charts where the weighting factors will vary according to individual needs.

In the past, decisions as to how many and what activities the center will pursue have been on a verbal, qualification theme. For example, rankings have ranged from passive (reacting to requests) through semiactive (keeping current with the immediate needs of the users) to active (anticipating information requirements). Activities have also been restricted to minimum, average, and maximum levels of effort.

The decision matrices in Exhibits 10 through 14 represent a departure from the traditional approach in that they are based on a numerical quantification plan. Various activity modes are listed across the chart and measured against a number of criteria down the chart. Weighting factors range from a high of ten to a nonexistent zero. For example, where the cost of an activity is high, the weight factor is low; but where the aid to the user is high, so is the numerical weight. In comparing the scores or totals applied to the different activities in the matrices, it should be noted that the weights may change, depending on the items already available for use in a com-

Exhibit 12. DECISION MATRIX FOR ANALYSIS AND SYNTHESIS

	Prepare Basic Bibliographic Identification	Make an Extract of the Article	Write an Abstract of the Contents	Evaluate the Material and State Critique in an Annotation	Classify Information for Storage and Retrieval	Index Data for Storage and Retrieval	Reference Other Material Pertinent to Information Under Consideration
Cost	8	6	4	10	10	10	10
Timeliness of Information	7	6	5	4	8	8	9
Ease of Operation	8	5	5	4	3	2	1
Training Required	8	4	3	1	1	1	1
Speed of Operation	9	7	5	2	4	3	2
Aid to User	4	6	8	10	10	10	10
Relevance of Material	5	6	7	9	9	9	10
TOTALS	49	40	37	40	45	43	43

Exhibit 13. DECISION MATRIX FOR MAINTENANCE

	Prepare a Card Catalog Manually	Print a Book Catalog	Develop EAM-Based Catalog	Produce EDP-Based Catalog	Maintain Hardbound Holdings	Store Material in Microform with Viewer and Printer Available	Bind Softbound Documents	Plan a Program for Updating Material	Purge Out-of-Date Material by a Planned Program
Cost	5	3	2	1	7	4	5	5	2
Ease of Operation	5	7	8	10	5	3	5	3	2
Training Required	4	8	3	2	6	3	2	1	1
Speed of Operation	6	9	9	10	4	7	4	3	3
Aid to User	7	8	9	10	5	7	5	10	10
Reliability	4	4	7	8	5	7	5	8	9
TOTALS	31	39	38	41	32	31	26	30	27

pany. The higher the total, the more desirable the activity. These matrices can be expanded for unique requirements of individual firms or to include additional criteria peculiar to certain industries.

IMPLEMENTING THE PLAN

The key to a successful implementation plan for an information center is top management backing. Without support from the top, the bottom will eventually fall out of the best of information centers.

The first phase of the implementation plan is the organizational establishment of the center somewhere in the corporate structure. The information center's appearance on an organization chart is evidence of executive management's at least tacit approval of its existence. A directive laying out the broad scope and responsibilities of the center is the next step in this first phase. Such a directive will

Exhibit 14. DECISION MATRIX FOR DISSEMINATION

	Circulate Holdings on Request	Route Pertinent Clippings and Ephemeral Materials	Route Journals and Periodicals on Request	Refer Clients to Sources of Information	Publish New-Acquisitions Bulletin	Publish List of Meetings and Call for Papers	Prepare Bibliographies	Conduct Retrospective Searches	Translate Into and From Foreign Languages	Establish Selective Dissemination of Information Program
Cost	5	6	7	5	7	8	9	9	10	10
Timeliness of Information	7	10	8	4	5	7	10	9	7	10
Ease of Operation	8	9	7	3	5	5	3	2	1	1
Training Required	8	7	9	3	4	3	1	1	1	1
Speed of Operation	7	9	7	5	7	7	4	2	5	3
Aid to User	7	8	8	4	7	8	9	10	10	10
Relevance of Material	7	10	9	3	4	9	10	10	8	10
TOTALS	49	59	55	27	39	47	46	43	42	45

permit the center staff to gather the bits of information lying about in unused files, desk drawers, and private collections and to construct the nucleus of an information center.

Phase 2 is the development stage. After seeing what material is already on hand, a purchasing plan must be undertaken to fill in the gaps of basic reference books, journals, and periodicals. As managers and operational personnel profit from services offered by the center, greater strides can be made to increase the holdings, enroll professional assistants, and add some automated techniques to increase the center's output.

Phase 3 is the stage where operations of various information centers are integrated into a single functioning group to provide one-stop information service for clients. In this phase, sharing facilities such as computer equipment is arranged and duplication of services is eliminated.

Phase 4 is the factoring in of feedback from users. Feedback can be obtained passively from oral and written compliments and complaints. Self-correcting information can also be acquired by conducting user surveys. It is this follow-through phase that makes an information center meaningful to its clients. It keeps the center abreast of the needs of its users and the potential requirements of the company.

The systems approach to information is applicable whether the information system contemplated is a one-man, one-room operation or an international computer-based network. Unless an organized approach is taken to meet information demands the results will be a needlessly expensive potpourri rather than a profitable resource.

The advantages of establishing an information center become more apparent to management when they are presented methodically and logically. The apprehension of management about installing expensive computers, costly microfilm equipment, and other high-priced facilities vanishes when the systems approach to information is followed.

A growth pattern from a basic reference information center to an automated information storage and retrieval operation is feasible when the information problem is approached from a systems outlook.

Without information, there cannot be coordination. Unless information circulates efficiently and effectively, it is our belief that coordination at the administration level and at the working scientific level will occur, if at all, only with greatest difficulty and expense.

—Hubert H. Humphrey

V

Organization of the Information Center

The position of the management and technical information center on a company's formal organization chart may be in any one of the following:

- At the corporate level with branches at the various divisions.
- As an autonomous department within a company.
- As part of the department it mainly serves; for example, engineering or R&D.
- As part of the administration or service department.

Some contend that the information center should be assigned to the area in which its services are least needed, the rationale behind this thought being that such a move would prevent bias or favoring the center's immediate environment in both holdings and services. In practice it has been found that unless the center operates as an autonomous department (as it does in some big companies), the closer it is to the majority of its customers the better. The close user-center relationship developed in such an organizational arrangement increases and improves the services, because the needs of the user are more readily determined and his demands can therefore be complied with more fully. Also, justification of budget requirements, expansion, and increased personnel are more easily explained to those most likely to benefit from the services than to some less interested group.

Once the position of the management and technical information center has been defined within the corporate structure, its own organizational chart should be drawn and its work flow diagrams should be prepared on the basis of the extent and intent of its functions.

The importance of the relationship of the information center with the other divisions of the company cannot be overemphasized. Although this chapter will dwell on the organization of the center itself, its manager should constantly keep in mind that the information center is organized to serve the rest of the company. He or his staff must regularly consult with members of the operating departments if the center is to keep abreast of user needs and encourage maximum use of the services it offers.

In small to medium-small companies, the information center usually starts as a company library. In the beginning it may occupy only a corner of a room where basic reference books are stored on a shelf, with a part-time clerk to keep the books in order and control circulation. As the company grows and the need for current technical and management information becomes evident, the company usually expands its part-time reference shelf facility, enlarging it to become a special library staffed with a full-time professional librarian. A well-thought-out acquisition program is then drawn up to provide the library with up-to-date material for its customers. Traditional library practices are followed: professional methods of cataloging, indexing, processing, and so on. As personnel within the company begin to use and benefit from the library and its services, the librarian is given an assistant to aid in processing increased holdings and to handle additional data. A clerk is now assigned to the growing library to aid in circulation control, filing, and typing. She is trained to assist in basic library processing functions. As the library increases its activities, its functions gradually become departmentalized, and additional professional and nonprofessional members are added to its staff.

In companies that depend on scientific and technical information or that require in-depth and continuing market research, the library is probably expanded into an information center. This conversion should not be an abrupt change, but should be part of a normal growth pattern. Management and technical literature research analysts are hired to analyze, synthesize, and summarize the material gathered by the library group. Bibliographers, research librarians, and other professionals with special skills are added to the staff. If automation of services seems feasible, a systems analyst takes his place among the personnel of the center.

Exhibit 15 is an organization chart showing a typical management and technical information center reflecting this growth pattern. As can be seen from the diagram, the information center does not replace the library function, but rather expands it and depends on it for material.

AREAS OF ACTIVITY

The information center's activities are divided into three major areas: management and administrative services, internal operating services, and external user services.

Management and administration. Management and administrative services include developing and implementing plans, policies, and standards consistent with the company's overall objectives. In addition, the administrative elements of the information center recommend policies to top management to help meet changing needs and handle emergency situations as they develop. Similarly, the management level of the center provides guidance to members of its own staff in line with established company policies and procedures. Through continuing review, old standards may be altered and new ones evolve. Also, periodic analyses of program plan accomplishments may indicate the need for changes. Management studies to identify and analyze problem areas, work measurement and simplification studies, maintenance of records, and compilation of statistics are also performed at the management level.

Establishing professional and nonprofessional personnel requirements and hiring staff with the requisite skills are responsibilities assigned to the administrative level. In line with personnel work, the administrator should supervise the work of his employees and de-

Exhibit 15. Organization Chart for a Management and Technical Information Center

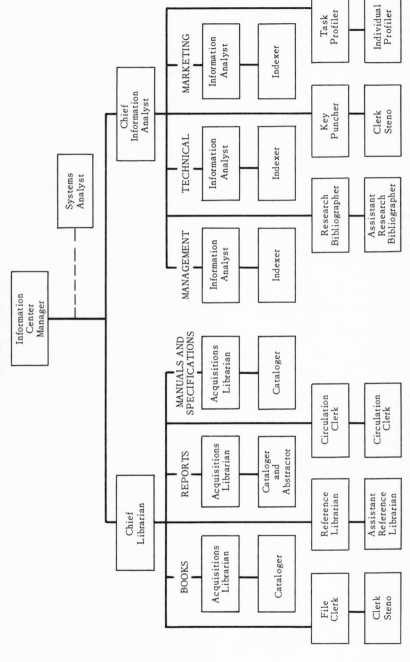

velop and prepare on-the-job instructional material and guidelines for his staff. Evaluating the center's operations in terms of user needs as well as for quality of performance also comes within the area of responsibility of the administrative level. Naturally, the management and administrative staff of the center determines and administers its budget. In line with planning, executing, and controlling expenditures are facilities planning, requisitioning supplies, and recommending equipment for maintaining and improving the center.

One of the most important and yet most frequently ignored obligations of the center's management and administrative personnel is the public relations function. Unless users, top managers, and external sources of information are kept informed of its accomplishments —what is currently taking place there and what its aims are—the information center will remain merely a depository rather than a disseminator of information.

Internal operation. The internal operating services of an information center break down into four major areas: acquiring and disposing of materials; cataloging and classifying the information; physically preparing the material for handling; and analyzing the data.

The selection of books, periodicals, reports, maps, patents, journals, and the rest for the center's collection should not be left solely to the judgment of its staff members but should reflect the suggestions and specialized knowledge contributed by company executives, scientists, engineers, and other specialists. Once the needs of users are determined, a policy should be formulated to allocate the available funds among the competing needs and claims of the various users. The center staff must keep abreast of current publishing activities and be aware of technical reviews, catalogs, and so on in order that a list of material may be prepared for purchase. Decisions should also be made as to what items need to be duplicated because of heavy demand. In the case of periodicals and journals, it is especially necessary that a retention policy be established.

However, a good information center also performs the action complementary to selection and acquisition: to discard and replace material. Needs change constantly, and acquisition and weeding practices should reflect these changes.

The decision-making process should not be permitted to overshadow the business aspects of acquisition when it comes to selecting material. The budget for new materials must be carefully controlled.

Money must be allocated for interlibrary loans, reprints, and material not obtainable through normal commercial channels. In addition, the person who orders material for the center must investigate the various means of obtaining items for the collection to determine the most economical one. Would it, for instance, be more efficient and practical to buy through a book dealer or directly from the publisher? Or would it be better to negotiate with a jobber when purchasing periodicals?

The cataloging, classifying, and indexing operations are professional tasks requiring that the practitioners have specialized technical knowledge. Once a classification format has been established it should be expanded and developed to meet changing needs. If either the Library of Congress system or the Dewey decimal system is chosen to classify books, the basic system must be maintained so that material can be located easily. Special classification schemes are available for maps, patents, and other nonconventional material.

Cataloging each item and recording the data in a main catalog file that describes each publication and identifies its unique features are mandatory for efficient operation. Determining correct subject headings for indexing the material requires the services of a professional cataloger and indexer who understands the subject matter thoroughly. In addition, the cataloger must understand the methods used by patrons to look for information in order to cross-reference the material to other subjects and disciplines in the most efficient and logical way. In the fields of science and technology, new terms are being created daily, and the cataloger must keep up with terminology changes to incorporate these new words into a meaningful catalog.

The physical preparation of the material after it is selected, acquired, and cataloged includes such activities as marking the spines of books with the correct call numbers, inserting pockets into books and periodicals to expedite charge-out procedures, and repairing and mending material as the need arises. Sending out a collection of unbound material for binding and having worn-out documents rebound also come within the scope of internal operating services.

The analysis, synthesis, and summarization of information by literature research analysts is the fourth area of internal operation. Here the analysts (sometimes called documentalists or technical information specialists) examine source materials, such as technical

Proprietary information which could help the organization obtain patents and maintain dominance in a product line must be carefully protected for the sake of both profit and prestige. Most companies establish policies which cover the protection and secrecy of such information. The information center staff should know these rules and be given the requisite authority to enforce them when the information is stored in the center.

Industrial security must be maintained to prevent a competitive business from marketing a product the company has developed but has not had time to put on the market. Also, should pricing data, overhead rates, and other financial information fall into the wrong hands, it might enable competition to underbid the company's proposals. The information center may be designated as the repository for such proprietary material. If so, its staff should be given the names of the individuals permitted access to this information.

Reproducing documents. In less sensitive areas, dissemination of information must be prompt, and the information must be in a form usable by the requester. The individual who needs the document should have access to it in hard copy format or microfilm from which prints can be made. A reproduction machine for duplicating portions of a document is a necessity, not merely a convenience in the center. And when the information is available only on a reel of microfilm or a microfiche card, a reader-printer is another essential adjunct.

Loan periods. Average loan periods are from one week to 30 days, depending on the items borrowed. Loans on current magazines are usually made for one week; new and popular books, reports, and journals are lent for two weeks; and other books and reports are lent for 30 days. Basic reference material such as encyclopedias, unabridged dictionaries, and engineering handbooks should not normally circulate unless duplicates are available in the information center.

Loan programs. Participating in an interlibrary loan program is essential to the firm needing information published in some of the more than 50,000 technical journals now being printed throughout the world each year. Few, if any, companies are so self-sufficient as to have available in one collection all the information required by their user populations. College and university libraries play an invaluable role by lending out-of-print books and furnishing copies of articles from periodicals in their collections to the industrial community. Out-of-print books and limited editions of papers are also available on loan from the Library of Congress to special company libraries.

REFERENCE SERVICES

Reference services are either passive or active. A *passive reference service* is one in which the information center acquires and makes available reference books, reports, and data; the user may examine these for the information he needs. Its operation is much the same as a reference room in a public library.

Active reference service is provided when a member of the staff locates the material for the requester, rather than have the requester find it for himself. Naturally, a fact retrieval service requires the service of a person more knowledgeable in the subject under search than is needed when the reference material is provided and the information is extracted by the requester. Facts may be culled from management reference materials such as reports, summaries, and documents, just as data are extracted in the conventional search from scientific and technical handbooks and journals.

There is also a *referral* aspect to reference service. When the information center itself does not have the material and cannot obtain it, if its location is known the user will be referred to the source. Such tracing of needed information saves untold hours of engineers' and managers' time and countless dollars that might otherwise be spent on duplicated research projects.

LITERATURE SEARCH

The intermediate stage between performing reference work and researching with information is literature searching. The literature search may be conducted at one of three levels: (1) current awareness search; (2) comprehensive search with reference to a specific problem; or (3) exhaustive search of current and historical files.

The purpose of a *current awareness search* is to alert the requester to the state of the art in a particular subject. A marketing survey may, in a sense, be considered a current awareness search. However, the term is usually applied to a survey of the latest events in a particular scientific discipline or technical area.

A *comprehensive search* made before the beginning of a major effort or task is usually conducted with the hope that all the information relating to the subject will be obtained. These point-of-reference searches are broad-based, however, and occasionally something from prior work in this field is not retrieved. Time and money dictate the thoroughness of the search. The collected information is given to the man who requested it; he sifts it and selects the references he will use.

When an *exhaustive retrospective search* is made, as much information as possible pertaining to the subject is collected. Before a company commits funds and manpower to undertaking basic research on a completely new item, it needs to be assured that the idea has not already been conceived and patented. This type of search is analogous to the housewife's search for dirt in her kitchen; she hopes she won't find any, but when she does she is psychologically rewarded for her search. Although managers and technical personnel may prefer to conduct the search themselves, the critical nature of the exhaustive search necessitates that professional literature researchers undertake this task. The discipline of indexing with vocabularies controlled by master thesauruses dictates that the best results from an exhaustive search will be achieved if the search is performed by the analysts most familiar with the methodology by which the material was indexed and classified originally.

RESEARCHING WITH INFORMATION

Upon completion of a literature search it may be discovered that the literature research analyst has been able to solve a technical problem, relieving the engineer or scientist of the need to resort to experimentation or releasing the manager from the need to make a value judgment. The acquiring, analyzing, synthesizing, and integrating of information from several sources may provide sufficient facts from which a conclusion can be drawn or a theorem can be verified without further effort. To provide this service, the information specialist must have both intensive and extensive knowledge of technical disciplines or subject matter areas related to the company's business. Researching with information implies not only arriving at conclusions beyond those reached by the individual authors investigated, but also discovering gaps in available research information. Usually a report similar to one filed at the end of a study or experiment is published, revealing the result of researching with information.

TRANSLATIONS

From a management point of view, a translation service supplied by the information center is becoming more and more a necessity. Companies have become increasingly international in their sales, purchases, acquisitions, and mergers. From a technical standpoint science has no geographical boundaries, and it has become a vital condition of industrial survival for a company's engineers and scientists to keep abreast of the engineering breakthroughs and new manufacturing techniques taking place in all parts of the world. If the information center has a staff translator, he should be sufficiently proficient in the foreign language to be able to read and interpret bibliographic citations in various fields and should be familiar with common reference materials used in translations, such as dictionaries and gazetteers. In a company involved in much foreign trade, the requirements for a translator should include a specialized vocabulary and a knowledge of the subject matter. In many of the subjects requiring translation, the terms are peculiar to that subject and are often so new they are not in a dictionary. Terminology in such fields as aerospace and oceanography change often because of the nature of the subject, and the translator must be able to produce the more accurate, up-to-date meaning.

Of course, translation services are available from outside sources. The Special Libraries Association directory on scientific translations lists 470 freelance translators and 87 translating firms in the United States and Canada. A semimonthly publication of the Clearinghouse for Federal Scientific and Technical Information, *Technical Translations,* lists scientific and technical translations from all known sources and indicates where copies may be ordered. This valuable announcement of translations is available through the U.S. Government Printing Office.

BIBLIOGRAPHIES

Bibliographies are usually compiled in an information center as the end result of a literature search, although demand bibliographies on both a comprehensive and selective basis are more and more often requested. Most information centers maintain continuing bibliographies in subject fields of interest to the company. The alert information center bibliographer anticipates the need for bibliographies and prepares them in advance of requests.

Bibliographies may be in the form of listings of books, periodicals, journals, reports, or articles arranged by author, subject, title, or date. Or they may include annotations evaluating and describing the contents of the listed items. Like the literature search the bibliography may be selective and comprehensive, or it may be exhaustive in approach. Few bibliographies are end items in themselves, but they provide a point of reference from which a more precise search may be conducted for the sources of information needed by the user.

INFORMATION SCOUTING

Information scouting consists of keeping abreast of who has what information where and referring the requester to the appropriate person and place in the company or outside it, or both. If a referral service is to be efficient, the information center must keep on file accurate, current data on the various collections, procedures, and key personnel in the major science and business information services in the United States. The personnel responsible for information scouting must be able to identify and evaluate the requester's needs accurately, in order to refer him to the various sources which may contain the information he is seeking. In addition, information center personnel must know the correct procedures for acquiring material or know how to gain access to it if it is not immediately available.

Information scouting has been developed to meet the need created by the generation of an enormous amount of information which is not being recorded or published in the usual communications media. Obviously, it is vital for a company to keep track of such information. Also, too often the time lag between the date an item of information is uncovered and the date it is published is so great that businessmen and scientists who need the data must be referred to the originating party before formal publication.

ABSTRACTS

Abstracting is the process of writing a summary of an article, report, journal, or similar publication so that the patron of an information center may quickly read a digest of the original material. Bibliographical details accompany the summary, giving the user enough information to identify the publication.

The person who prepares the abstract must have comprehensive knowledge of the subject matter he is summarizing. The author himself may provide the simple or descriptive abstract, whose purpose is simply to advise the reader that the material exists and to supply enough information to enable him to judge if its contents are pertinent to his needs. An analytical abstract breaks down the contents of the document and relates it to other material within the same subject field. A critical abstract goes one step further, evaluating the material as to validity, pertinence, relevance, and significance. The subject matter and the needs of the information center's customers will determine the treatment of the abstract.

Some information centers whose customers are mainly management personnel divide their abstracts into two classes: descriptive and informative. The descriptive abstract gives the title of the article and supplies enough information to help the manager decide whether he should read the complete item. The informative abstract is so complete in its concise format that the reader does not have to refer to the original for the information he is seeking.

The extract is another form of abstract information. Here the information specialist extracts key sentences and phrases from the original publication or management report and places them in a logical order. This selection of quoted portions of the source material allows the user to judge the style and theme of the material. In a sense, an extract is an author's summary abstract prepared by an information specialist. An annotation to the extract is helpful for evaluating the material and deciding if management should pursue it further.

Abstract service. Besides preparing abstracts of company-generated material and externally originated publications, the information center may elect to subscribe to some of the nearly 2,000 abstract and index services. These secondary publications are usually oriented toward a particular scientific or technical discipline, although a few specialize in management information, a product line, or specific tasks with interdisciplinary requirements.

Subscriptions to pertinent abstract and index services should be maintained and the publications made available to all management and technical personnel. Without the services of secondary journals such as *Chemical Abstracts, Mathematical Reviews,* and *Engineering Index,* thousands of items of valuable information would be lost in the mountain of technical literature published daily. Managers seeking information about a business topic have been greatly aided by referring to H. W. Wilson Company's *Business Periodicals Index* or *Readers' Guide to Periodical Literature.*

Announcement services. Related to the field of abstracts and extracts are announcement services such as the Government Printing Office's *Selected List of Government Publications* and the *Gazette* published by the U.S. Patent Office. Like the various aspects of abstracting, announcement services range in depth from simple title listings to full-blown critical abstracts and content summaries.

MEETING ANNOUNCEMENTS AND CALL FOR PAPERS

In addition to keeping an agenda of all important meetings and visits of substance scheduled within the company, the information center should maintain a calendar of meetings, symposia, and colloquia related to the interests of the company.

Informing both management and technical personnel of calls for papers is a service for which the information center should be responsible. Using the printed word to keep aware of the current trends in the various management and scientific disciplines is a weak substitute for dialogue between informed individuals. The publication of papers presented at technical gatherings not only adds to the storehouse of knowledge in a particular field; it also increases the prestige of the company as a leader in that field. Since the primary purpose of an information center is to keep up with the flow of information, it is only natural that this method of transmitting knowledge should be among its activities.

After a conference of interest to the company has taken place, the center should make every effort to obtain the proceedings of the meeting. In addition, it should take advantage of a new trend that has recently developed, whereby symposium papers are published before the conference so that those who attend can study the presentation beforehand and discuss its contents with the speaker. These preprints should be acquired by the information center for the management and technical staff of the company.

Transcriptions of informal conferences and discussions which take place in the company should be submitted to the information center and there be properly classified and indexed for later reference. Too frequently a manager has strained his memory trying to recall a chance remark or comment heard at a meeting that he now vitally needs to remember in order to incorporate it in a plan. The record of that meeting would be available in the center if transcripts were made of such meetings. Also, charts, graphs, and other visual material used in various presentations should accompany the documentation. These visual aids can be reduced photographically and filed with the meeting notes.

INFORMATION CENTER PUBLICATIONS

As part of its responsibility for the flow of information within the company, the center should inform its users of the various holdings, new acquisitions, updated bibliographies, calendar of meetings, and similar information pertinent to company needs. These announcements should not appear sporadically, but should be published on a regular schedule. A list of titles of the internally generated reports and documents entering the system will alert personnel to those areas in which there is activity within the organization.

By cataloging reports acquired from another company for one employee, the center provides a useful service to other employees who may not have been aware of the existence of the material. Listing a new acquisition may prevent both duplication of research within the company and reordering of material for someone who did not know it had already been purchased.

As mentioned earlier, publishing a calendar of management and technical briefings held in the company, as well as of symposia and professional meetings held outside the company, keeps personnel alerted to these activities in their fields. Such a schedule also aids advertising and marketing personnel who may wish to set up displays at such meetings. And, of course, the company recruiters will find such lists helpful in their search for professional personnel and employees with specialized skills.

Anticipating the need for and publishing up-to-date bibliographies and announcing their availability may save many days of delay in waiting for information after it has been requested. Sometimes, just this small amount of lead time is all that is needed to give a manager or scientist the edge over a competitor.

These publications need not be elaborate or expensive. A simple mimeographed or ditto copy of an announcement will fill most requirements adequately. On the other hand, the lack of such publications can prove a costly "saving" if some employees are working with less than complete knowledge of their tasks.

USER ORIENTATION

In conjunction with the publication of material about its changing collection of data, the information center has an obligation to inform its users about the various services it has available and how such tools as card catalogs, indexes, and abstract services can best be used.

All new management and technical employees should be invited to attend an information center orientation meeting. To those who are familiar with the workings of an information center, the session will be a refresher course. And when employees who did not know of the advantages to be derived by using the center become aware of these benefits, they will be better able to use all available resources in doing their assigned tasks.

Also, such orientation sessions eliminate confusion and misunderstanding regarding the dissemination of limited access documents, circulation loan periods, and other policies and procedures. The company also benefits from fresh ideas and suggestions these new employees may offer. Such ideas are worthy of study for possible incorporation into the present way of doing things. A good presentation by the center staff will inspire an appreciation for the professional skills required to operate the center in supporting the many needs of the company, as well as for the variety of services that it may provide employees.

Everything that a manager does ultimately comes down to decision making, and the science of management is the art of organizing facts for the decision-making process. In the management business facts are like ammunition to the infantry and like gasoline to the aviator. Without facts operation is not possible, and the organization and the assimilation of facts is the area where the good manager exercises his greatest artistry.

—THOMAS J. RUDDEN, JR.

VII

Qualitative and Quantitative Growth Patterns

As a company grows, correspondingly greater demands are made for more and better information to help exercise control, solve problems, and make decisions so as to insure future growth and development. This success spiral must be reflected by the information center as it takes over the job of manipulating information into a format meaningful to management.

Analysis and synthesis of raw data increase in importance as the activities of the information center expand. Abstracting, extracting, indexing, and classifying information for retrieval by management and technical personnel become necessities as information proliferates. The larger scope of activities creates a need for personnel who are qualified to handle certain specialized tasks.

CURRENT AWARENESS PROGRAM

When plans are made to add key personnel to the staff of the information center, these should include staffing for a current awareness program—a program which should be inaugurated as soon as the center is formally opened. In the beginning this may be a simple courtesy operation, with members of the staff mentally keeping an interest profile of particular users. When a literature researcher examines incoming data, for example, he sometimes encounters information that may be meaningful to a particular client; as part of the informal current awareness program, he informs the client that the material is available.

The next step is to formalize this program. Arrangements are made to send automatically to the employees lists of the contents of selected magazines, reprints of journal articles, and new reports in their particular fields of interest. Such automatic dissemination of information is possible only if the center has advance knowledge of the interest in the applicable subject matter and if the center's employees personally know the users of the center.

The Institute for Scientific Information in Philadelphia publishes *Current Contents,* which contains tables of contents from important journals in various specialized areas of interest. Circulating this magazine or others similar to it to interested individuals within the organization alerts them to the existence of articles they may wish to obtain and read in full.

SELECTIVE DISSEMINATION OF INFORMATION

Selective dissemination of information (SDI) is the term applied to the integration into a formal system of the courtesy service provided by a current awareness program. The information center establishes and maintains a field-of-interest register on each individual participating in the program. This profile of users' needs is formulated on the basis of interviews and questionnaires about their past assignments, present requirements, and anticipated future efforts. As the information facility acquires new items of information, the users' field-of-interest profiles are matched against this material. The SDI subscriber is automatically notified of all newly acquired material that matches his profile. A feedback system is built into the program; the recipient of the announcement is requested to return a card signifying whether the information is not relevant; relevant, but not needed; or relevant, send document.

If the SDI user receives a number of announcements of material that is not relevant to his needs, his profile is modified to reflect his requirements more precisely. One objective of the program is to keep the user informed of what is going on in his field without deluging him with data; by the same token, the other extreme (providing no information) is to be avoided. The employee's new assignments —and related new interests—can be incorporated into the profiles when the information group is notified of such events. Exhibit 16 is a flow chart of a typical SDI program operated manually.

The SDI program can be converted into an automated system by having the indexing terms of the profiles keypunched on cards, as are the indexing terms of new documents. Documents and profiles can be matched mechanically and then handled in a sorter; the user is later informed of the matched item. The most sophisticated method of handling is by computerizing the program. The matching takes place on magnetic tapes, and abstracts of the matched items are retrieved and printed out along with the user's name and address. This SDI abstract card is sent along to the user. Automation and computerization of information center services will be discussed in a later chapter.

Key-Word-in-Context

Key-word-in-context (KWIC) is another service that may be offered to information center users as the number of customers increases and the center's services become computerized. KWIC is a permuted index; the key words in the title are permuted, then aligned in alphabetical order in a specific column on a page. Insignificant words such as articles and prepositions are not alphabetized as key words. As an example, the title of this book would appear in a KWIC listing as follows:

Exhibit 16. SELECTIVE DISSEMINATION OF INFORMATION
FLOW CHART

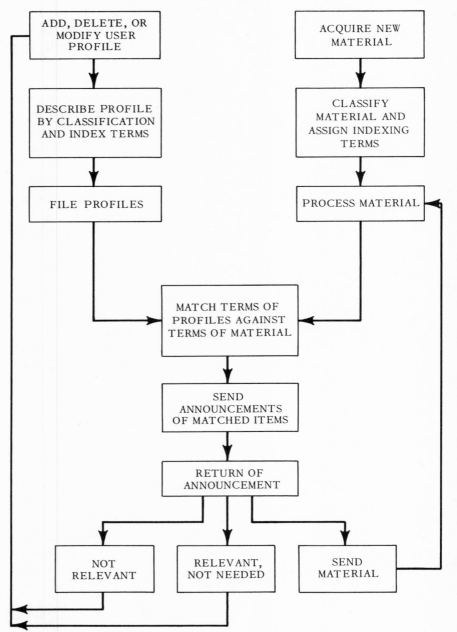

Management's Hidden	*Asset.* The Information Center:
Asset. The Information	*Center:* Management's Hidden
Center: Management's	*Hidden* Asset. The Information
Hidden Asset. The	*Information* Center: Management's
The Information Center:	*Management's* Hidden Asset.

The advantage of listing new titles of material in this fashion is that it is quick and inexpensive. The disadvantage becomes apparent when titles are not meaningful or do not accurately reflect the contents of the material. Of course, the KWIC approach may be used with the abstract or the text of the document, although in most cases it is applied only to the title.

CLASSIFYING AND INDEXING

From appraisals of the three examples cited for improving the basic information center services, it should be obvious that the foundation for all systems is a meaningful classification scheme combined with thorough indexing of subject matter.

Classifying is the process of arranging subjects into groups on the basis of similarities. The Dewey decimal system used in most public libraries in this country is a typical classification scheme. The type and depth of information being handled by the information center will determine the classification scheme best suited for use by a particular group. Many organizations develop their own systems which meet their particular needs. Whatever scheme is used, it should be flexible enough to adapt to all changes occasioned by the company's changing interests.

Indexing is the assignment of words and terms to indicate the contents of the material. This involves making a detailed subject analysis of the material to identify its essential features and to select the words by which the material may be retrieved in the future. The original terms used by the writer of the material may not be the best ones to use for indexing if they are not in normal use or universally understood. The research analyst must keep up with current terminology changes in a subject field, the frequency with which words occur, and the relationship between concepts of the subject matter. Unless the researcher indexes the material with both current and

Exhibit 17. COORDINATE INDEXING SYSTEM

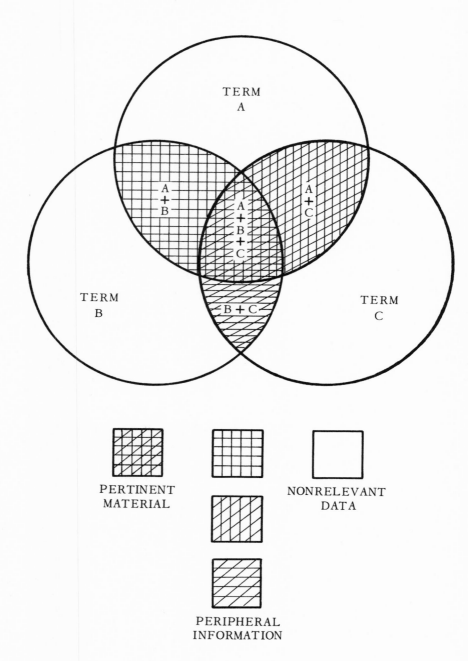

future users in mind, the information may become lost in the accumulation of data that builds up daily in the center. The indexer must also be familiar with the search patterns used by people looking for the information, since the idea behind an index is to indicate the existence of the material to anyone searching for it.

Such typical index entries as title, originator (writer and company name), control number, conventional subject headings, and contract numbers are helpful guideposts for locating material. Concept indexing—in which the ideas contained in the material are identified and described—gives the user a more efficient system to aid him in his search. Describing information by terms which represent unit concepts requires that the indexer have a vocabulary control which discriminates between similar words and indicates the connection between related words. Also, the limits or scope of the concept must be described so that only material which fits within the scope or meaning of the term will be placed in the index.

A thesaurus is a reference authority for terminology which, by a series of cross references and explanatory notes, allows the indexers to handle the material in the same way. It is used to control the terminology to provide consistency and insure validity of analysis. The Engineers Joint Council *Thesaurus of Engineering Terms* and the *Chemical Engineering Thesaurus* are two of the more comprehensive technical thesauruses currently being published.

Processing information under such controlled terminology conditions permits coordinated indexing, which is the correlation of two or more descriptive terms or concepts. It eliminates much peripheral information that is not germane to the subject under consideration. For example, a manager who wants information about the profit and loss statement of a competitor would not need to search vast files of information regarding the company being investigated; nor would he have to examine all the available files on profit and loss statements. Only documents containing both the name of the company and the key term "profit and loss statement" would be retrieved from the collection of material. If more specific data were needed, more terms could be used in the search—history of acquisitions, new product lines, and so on. Naturally, using a greater number of terms will insure that a greater amount of relevant information is forthcoming. Conversely, the amount of material diminishes as the qualifications for retrieval increase. Exhibit 17 shows a coordinate indexing system in which three terms are used. At the point where the three terms converge will be found the material most applicable to the information being sought. Peripheral information will probably be obtained where two terms overlap. It is unlikely that worthwhile data will be found in nonintersecting areas.

In more sophisticated methods of retrieval, Boolean logic can be applied to the indexing terms; such combinations as the following can thus be used to obtain management and technical information that is apropos of the assignment at hand.

- Retrieve only when A *and* B appear together.
- Retrieve either A *or* B.
- Retrieve A only when it does *not* appear with B.

For example, the request could be for information only when the terms fuel and injection appear together, or for information on either fuel or injection, or for information on fuel when it does not appear with the term injection.

Besides such logic, certain weighting factors and techniques (such as links and roles) separate the pertinent data even more distinctly from the mass of information accumulated in the files. However, no matter how sophisticated a system for recovering information may be, prompt, efficient retrieval depends on accurate and complete indexing when the material is first analyzed for content.

There may be some substitute for hard facts and factual information, but if there is, I have no idea what it can be. It certainly isn't rumor or opinion that has been camouflaged as fact. In order to succeed in any "deal," project or endeavor, the businessman must assemble all the available pertinent hard facts and study and analyze them himself. There's nothing wrong in asking the opinions of others and in taking them into consideration. The mistake lies in accepting and following other people's advice blindly, in accepting their opinions without first determining if they are backed up by facts. This is one of the first lessons young businessmen and executives should learn—or they will find themselves being taught it the hard way.

—J. PAUL GETTY

VIII

What Price Information?

In establishing the budget for a management and technical information center, costs fall into two major categories—initial costs and operating expenditures.

Initial cost. Under initial costs, such basic items as capital equipment, purchase of the basic collection of books and reports, subscriptions to periodicals, and salaries are taken under consideration.

Operating expenses. Once the center is established, the operating budget should cover funds for replacing old equipment, buying new equipment, adding to the basic collection of books and reports, and maintaining subscriptions to periodicals. Funds should be allocated for purchasing abstracting services and similar publications as the information group expands the scope of its activities. Money should be set aside for outside services such as translating and special retrospective searches. A travel budget should be allotted so that staff members may attend seminars and professional meetings. A supply budget for items such as binding materials, Library of Congress catalog cards, and expendable material must also be established. The budget must include provision for salaries and merit increases for personnel. And additional costs for rental or purchase of data processing or computer equipment must be considered if plans include introduction of automation into the information center's operations.

Budget ratios. It is more useful to look at the information center's budget from a ratio point of view than from the standpoint of actual

Exhibit 18. BUDGET RATIOS

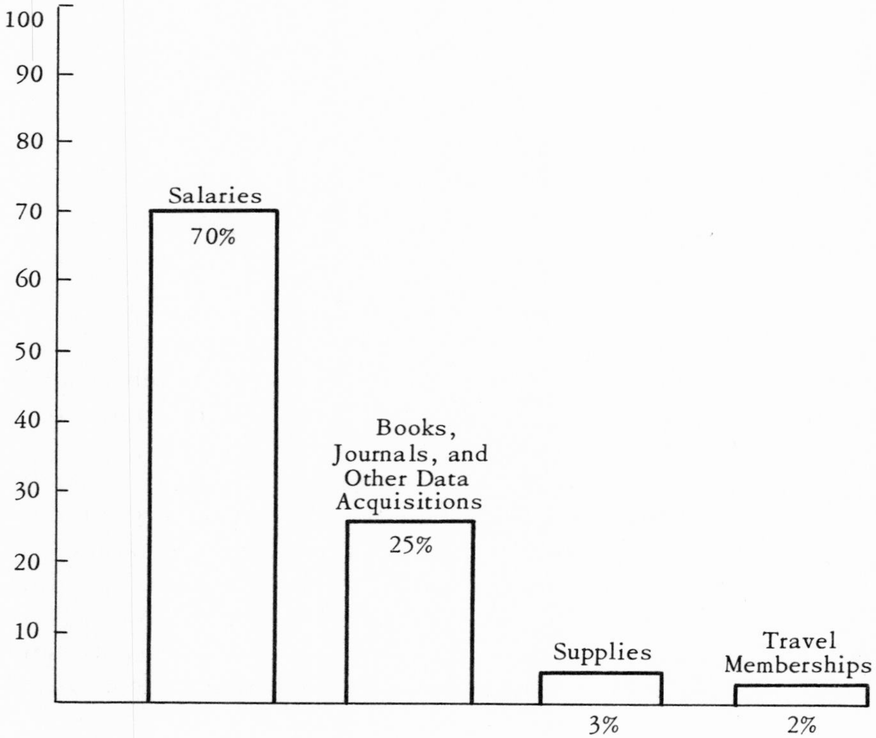

dollars. Exhibit 18 shows the budget ratios for salaries, acquisitions, supplies, and travel and membership dues.

Wages and salaries. The expenditures for personnel include the pay of both professional and nonprofessional help. Table I gives the range of salaries for the various positions in a typical management and technical information center. Factors such as geographical location, level of responsibility, size of the center, scope of assignment, and knowledge requirements may shift the value ranges upward or downward.

Table I. WAGES AND SALARIES

Title of Position	Salary Range
Information center director	$12,500–$22,500
Chief information specialist	8,650– 18,580
Chief librarian	7,220– 15,850
Information specialist	7,220– 15,850
Librarian	6,050– 13,450
Information specialist associate	6,050– 13,450
Translator	6,000– 13,000
Librarian associate	5,000– 11,300
Secretary	5,000– 6,800
Clerk-typist	4,500– 5,700

Merit increases of approximately 6 percent per year are considered average. Naturally, such factors as quality of work, potential, work skills, and self-improvement will bias this percentage and frequency either way.

Cost of acquiring data. Material comes to the information center in many forms and from many sources: books, periodicals, indexing and abstracting services, technical reports, lecture cards, and so on. The data may be furnished on a no-charge or postage-only basis as in the case of some government reports or trade association material; they may exceed $1,000 per year for a single item, such as *Chemical Abstracts* and other excellent indexing services.

The prices of scientific and technical books have increased steadily for the past decade—in 1967 the average price is $12 to $15. Business and economic books cost about $10 each. When the information center is organized, the first books purchased for its collection will fall in the category of basic references pertinent to the interests of the company. In nontechnical areas, the nucleus of a collection should consist of recognized encyclopedias, an unabridged dictionary, a comprehensive atlas, *Poor's Register of Corporations, Directors and Executives, United States and Canada, Thomas' Register of American Manufacturers,* applicable "Who's Who" books, and Wilson's *Business Periodicals Index* and *Readers' Guide to Periodical Literature.* The initial investment in books should be about $3,500, with a minimum annual book budget of between $1,000 and $1,500 to allow for the purchase of approximately 100 new books.

Unquestionably, books are an excellent medium for reference material. But the dynamic company that intends to keep up with what is happening in technical fields and in the business world must depend to a large extent on periodicals, which do not have the publication time lag of books. (At least six months must elapse after the publisher receives a manuscript before the book appears in the stalls.) But just as the price of books has risen continually, so too has the price of periodicals escalated. On the average, an annual subscription to a scientific or technical journal will cost about $20, while business periodicals cost in the neighborhood of $10 per year. A medium-size company in the research and development business should subscribe to a minimum of 250 periodicals at the ratio of three technical journals to each business periodical. Thus an annual budget of $4,370 for periodicals is an average expenditure.

The need for back issues of periodicals is an item often overlooked when the budget for the information center is established. In the center that plans to prepare bibliographies and conduct retrospective searches, complete journal collections are particularly important. Even though some needed issues may be out of print, services are available which will locate and sell those items in the original. Other companies may also have the material available in some form such as microfilm or microprint copies. An annual allocation of $3,000 for back issues is average.

Subscriptions to secondary publications such as abstracting and indexing services should run about the same as or higher than the amount allotted to current periodical subscriptions. Typical subscription prices for such services are: *Physical Review*, $50 a year; *Mathematical Reviews*, $180 annually for 12 issues; *The Engineering Index*, $100 for the annual volume alone plus $250 for 12 monthly publications. *Chemical Abstracts*, a biweekly publication, costs $1,200 a year. There are some excellent government publications available free of charge to Department of Defense contractors. These include the *Technical Abstract Bulletin* and the NASA *Scientific and Technical Aerospace Report,* which costs $33 annually to non-NASA contractors.

Although most information centers purchase books and periodicals and subscribe to secondary publications, the major source of information for the industrial firm is the technical report. Most of this material is available at no cost or at a nominal handling charge. The alert information center director keeps in touch with report-producing agencies and acquires the data applicable to his company's needs. Certain government agencies regularly produce technical and scientific reports, all of which are listed in the monthly *U.S. Government Research & Development Reports.* The monthly *Catalog of Government Publications* covers Congressional hearings, documents, and reports by agency. Similar publications are issued by trade associations, universities, and nonprofit organizations.

The information center should make arrangements to receive automatically the pertinent material that is free, and it should set aside about $1,000 per year to cover the acquisition of those reports for which a charge is made. If certain agencies seem to be the major sources for these reports, it may be practical to establish an account with each agency; as purchases are made they are deducted from the initial deposit. The Government Printing Office, for example, makes such an arrangement available, as do some of the larger technically oriented universities.

A portion of the budget should be earmarked for translation of material that cannot be handled by the linguistic talents of the regular staff. Approximately $300 per year should be allocated for buying translations filed at the Library of Congress or the John Crear Library or for subcontracting translations of original documents. Translations of most European languages are available at the rate of $10 per thousand words; translations of the less familiar languages such as Chinese, Japanese, and Russian cost about $15 a thousand words. Obviously, the amount of money set aside for translations will be determined by the international aspects of the business, the technology of its industry, and the number and importance of breakthroughs in related business and science that take place in various countries.

Table II presents a summary of the initial and annual allocations for acquisitions in a typical information center.

Table II. Budget Allocations for Acquisitions

	Initial	Annual
Books	$3,500	$1,000–$1,500
Periodicals	4,370	4,370
Back issues	—	3,000
Abstracting and indexing services	4,500	4,500
Technical reports	1,000	1,000
Translations	300	300

Supplies. In the first year of its operation, the information center director should plan to spend close to $300 for supplies; each year thereafter these expenses should run about half that amount. Such standard office supplies as scissors, paper clips, stationery, and postage, as well as items peculiar to the information center such as chargeout cards, book mending material, and contracts for binding periodicals and rebinding books, are included in this budget.

Travel and membership dues. Management and technical information center personnel should regularly attend seminars pertinent to their work, exchange ideas with fellow professionals at symposia, and present papers at information organization colloquia. Most of these meetings take place in New York, Los Angeles, and Washington, D.C., although excellent professional meetings are held throughout the United States. Of course, the amount of money allocated for travel will be influenced by the geographical proximity of a company to the three major meeting areas.

Membership dues in the three professional societies associated most with management and technical information centers are as follows:

American Documentation Institute	$20
American Library Association	$6 to $50 depending on income
Special Libraries Association	$20

Membership in scientific and technical and management associations should be considered, particularly for the information specialists on the staff.

Equipment. The initial expenditure for equipping an information center is basically a nonrecurring capital expense and therefore should not be included in the budget ratios. However, as the information group expands its services, holdings, and space, money should be set aside to provide the equipment to enable the staff to cope with their increased undertakings. The original investment in equipment should allow for a five-year growth pattern. The basic equipment needed to establish an information center is as follows:

- 500 three-feet-wide bookshelves.
- 250 three-feet-wide periodical shelves.
- 50 periodical display shelves.
- 20 five-drawer file cabinets.
- 1 microfilm cabinet.
- 1 unabridged dictionary stand.
- 1 map case.
- 1 microfilm reader-printer.
- 1 duplicating machine capable of reproducing bound volumes.
- 1 slide cabinet.
- 1 newspaper rack.
- 12 reading chairs.
- 3 reading tables.
   desks, chairs, and typewriters for the information center personnel.

An original outlay of between $5,000 and $10,000 will be needed to equip the center adequately. An additional $1,000 a year should be set aside for minor additions, maintenance, and repair of equipment.

Because information about what is going on is necessary for making decisions, improvement in scientific information systems is sometimes represented as a panacea for bad management of research and development. Though it is true that poor management can and does occur with the best of communication systems, poor communication almost always leads to bad management. . . . Information is only one of the many tools that the manager of research and development must have; the use to which he puts the information—indeed, the diligence and responsibility he shows in unearthing needed information—is determined only by his own skill as a manager.

—SCIENCE, GOVERNMENT, AND INFORMATION

IX

Determining the Return on Investment

In the preceding chapter we discussed some of the investments a company must make to begin acquiring and disseminating information within its organization. This chapter deals with the return on these investments.

It may be unfair to place an arbitrary dollar value on the information provided by the information center, as such a statement might tend to give an unfair advantage to the center. Dollars saved in averting duplication of experiments, profits earned from a supplied fact that resulted in development of a best-selling product line, increased company earnings realized from a merger with a firm that was first heard of in a business report, could all be totaled and presented as "return on investment."

An alternative way of looking at return on investment that seems preferable to the dollar value approach is to establish criteria and measure the information center's performance against those standards. The nine basic criteria by which we may measure an information center's performance are (1) timeliness, (2) completeness, (3) accuracy, (4) recall, (5) relevance, (6) simplicity, (7) flexibility, (8) economy, and (9) user orientation.

Timeliness. No decision should be delayed because information is lacking. Information is valueless unless it is available when needed. Actually, timeliness is a two-headed coin for the managers and technical personnel who require information. First, the timeliness or up-to-dateness of the information itself must be considered. Second, the time that elapses between the request for information and its presentation to the client must also be taken into account.

In the first instance, not all information need be current—just as not all members of an organization work on a real-time basis. Those who deal with administrative and control functions often need up-to-the-minute cost and schedule data upon which to base their decisions. On the other hand, those who work in laboratories and in manufacturing and research areas need state-of-the-art information on developments that have taken place within the past few years; in some instances they may need to search the literature from as much as 20 years earlier in order to trace the pattern of development of a particular item. The time lag in acquiring information after it has been generated as a document or a fact should pose no problem as long as the system is geared to feed new data automatically into the information organization as it develops. An alert information center staff with strong management backing will insure the timeliness of the material the center provides.

The second aspect of timeliness, the span after the center is called on to search out the information until it is actually produced, is a criterion containing several variables. Whether the center is automated or manually operated will have a bearing on the speed of reply. How well the question was presented to the center will also have an impact on the speed of information retrieval. Many times the search for information must be repeated because the original question was not clear. The crux of timeliness in this context is whether the requested material can be provided within a time span in which it can be utilized. If the delay in receiving the information is excessive, a decision may have to be made without benefit of the data, or duplicate effort may have to be undertaken.

Promptness in supplying information may well be the factor determining whether the information center remains in existence or is shelved as an inefficient overhead function. If the users receive poor service from the center, they will lose confidence in it and turn to other sources for data. Since executives, chief engineers, and scientists have a professional requirement as well as a responsibility to keep informed of events in their own and related fields, the information group likewise has an obligation to deliver the material to these people when they need it. The ability of the system to react speedily and efficiently to users' schedules is mandatory. Excessive retrieval time will never be tolerated for long. Delivering the most accurate and complete information late is worse than delivering no information at all; neither benefits the client. Man-hours lost while waiting for information from the center represent a debit in the center's ledger. Money, time, and talent saved by data produced on time can be posted to the credit column.

Completeness. The completeness of the information delivered to clients is another measure which can be applied to the functioning information center. Completeness has two dimensions: the depth and the breadth of the information.

Depending on the requester's needs and the time available, the depth of information supplied may be as elementary as a simple bibliography indicating the existence of possibly applicable material —or as complex and thorough as an analysis and synthesis of pertinent material, published as a state-of-the-art report.

The breadth of the information supplied must be such as to assure the client that coverage is complete; that consideration was given both to obviously pertinent data and to peripheral data that could have a bearing on the problem. Incomplete information may at times be as costly as no data at all. Wrong conclusions, inconsistent inferences, and erroneous implications may be the result of partial facts. Thus both the scope and detail of the services provided by the information center are valid standards by which to appraise performance. One pitfall must be avoided when evaluating completeness: the danger of supplying data too comprehensive for the task at hand.

This must be taken into account when the center's performance is evaluated. Researchers should not spend thousands of dollars seeking an answer when the effort for which the search is being made will involve only a hundred dollars.

Accuracy. Accuracy and validity of data comprise the third criterion to be applied when judging yield on investment. No matter how timely, prompt, and complete the information supplied may be, if it is not accurate it is less than worthless. Items in the cost, scheduling, and inventory areas are more prone to be inaccurate and invalid than are the data produced to aid a scientist or engineer; the constantly changing inputs to management information increase the probability of error, and therefore great care should be taken in handling these data to insure their accuracy. Weeding out documents and purging files of outdated information that has been nullified by the development of new data will aid in keeping information accurate, but checks must be applied to insure the validity of the material produced. Intrinsic to this concept of accuracy is reliability. The facts presented to the clients may be accurate, based on the input of information, but the reliability of this original source material is an additional concern of the information specialist who evaluates the incoming data.

Recall. The recall ratio is closely associated with the criterion of completeness. This is a quantitative measure of effectiveness used in most computer-based storage and retrieval systems, though it may also be applied to centers that are not automated. The recall ratio is the number of relevant documents or items retrieved out of the total number of relevant documents in the entire collection of material. Mathematically it can be expressed as follows:

$$\text{Recall ratio} = \frac{\text{number of relevant documents retrieved}}{\text{number of relevant documents in collection}}$$

What is being measured here is the amount of relevant information actually recalled out of all the relevant information in the system. It does not take into consideration the amount of irrelevant information recalled erroneously. Care must be taken that the staff of the center doesn't fall into the trap of providing quantity in preference to quality. Supplying a user with an overabundance of information that he cannot possibly assimilate can prevent him from absorbing what is truly important.

Relevance. Of vital concern must be the amount of time consumed by the inquirer in screening out irrelevancies. The need is for better—not more—information. Thus the next criterion, relevance, must be considered along with the recall ratio. The relevance ratio is the number of pertinent documents out of the number of documents retrieved. It may be equated as follows:

$$\text{Relevance ratio} = \frac{\text{number of pertinent documents retrieved}}{\text{number of documents retrieved}}$$

This is sometimes referred to as the precision ratio, since it establishes which items are precisely germane to the material needed. There is an inverse relationship between the recall and the relevance ratios. As the quantity of documents or facts produced from the store of information increases, their relevance to the question at hand tends to decrease.

Conversely, as the material produced becomes more precise and specific in its application to the problem, the number of items produced decreases. Whereas the recall ratio is quantitatively oriented, the relevance ratio is an indicator of quality.

In using a combination of recall and relevance ratios in evaluating the performance of an information center, the following matrix is helpful in giving a quantitative measure to a qualitative criterion.

	Relevant Information	Not Relevant Information
Information retrieved	1	2
Information not retrieved	3	4

If the information was retrieved and is relevant to the question being considered, it would be regarded as a hit and placed in Quadrant 1. The information that was retrieved but found to be not relevant in solving the problem would be accounted for in the second quadrant as a mistaken retrieval. Relevant material that was not retrieved would be shown as a miss in Quadrant 3. Correct screening of irrelevant material so that it was not retrieved would be tallied in the fourth quadrant as a positive rejection. When many items fall in the first and fourth quadrants, a good system is being used. On the other hand, when an unusually large amount of material falls into the second and third quadrants, too much useless information is being offered users of the center, or a significant quantity of important data is being lost. Exhibit 19 is a graphic representation of the relationship between the recall and relevance ratios.

Simplicity. Simplicity of operation is one of the criteria by which the value of the center may be justly measured. Too many administrative roadblocks or too much red tape for staff members and users to contend with results in an inefficient system and will cause users to turn to other sources for information. It is a well-known fact of

Exhibit 19. RELATIONSHIP OF RELEVANCE TO RECALL RATIOS

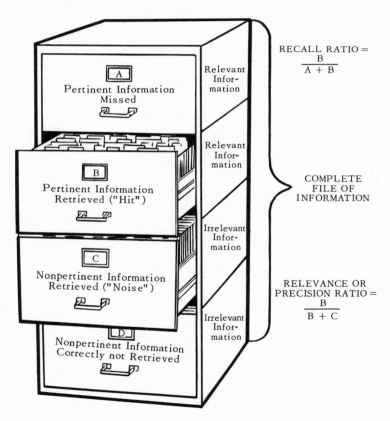

human behavior that people follow the line of least resistance to achieve their goals. If it is easier for an employee to bypass the center to acquire information he will use other and more convenient avenues to achieve his ends.

Personnel requirements and training demands will also indicate whether the center is a simple or a complex undertaking. If the operations of the information center must be undertaken only by professional manpower, the center's processes have become too sophisticated. A ratio of two nonprofessionals to each professional on the staff is average for most such organizations. Also, the various tasks within the center should not be so esoteric that only specialized training on the job will provide the needed skills. Unique systems that require unique staffing will soon be out of business because the needed skilled personnel will not be available. Potential users will be eliminated because they are uncomfortable in the unconventional atmosphere of the sophisticated information center. People prefer to use more conventional methods in a more conventional environment in which they feel secure. An information center is a service within a larger organization; and when one group—the information center—has to be served more than the organization it serves, it has lost its reason for being.

Flexibility. As new sources of information are derived and new demands are placed on the information center, the system should be flexible enough to cope with additional requirements. Further, the information organization should be able to meet the changing needs of a dynamic company as old products are replaced by new items and as marketing areas shift.

The center should be adaptable to the systems used by other such groups. This uniformity in system and procedures does not preclude the use of creativity in services; it does permit greater ease of operation and extensive participation in national and trade association information networks.

The center should be loose from both an input and an output point of view. It should be able to receive material presented in any format: documents, books, reports, slides, microfilms, photos, and so on. Similarly, the output to the client should be in a form usable by him: bibliographic references, abstracts, actual copies, or graphic displays.

An information center that has an inflexible system and is unable to meet the needs of all levels and groups in the company has severe limits to its usefulness. An information organization must be service-oriented and able quickly to meet the company's demands for a complete spectrum of information.

Economy. The management and technical information center must pay its way. It must offer a service less expensive than is available from any other source. In appraising the economics of the center, the costs of establishing and operating it, the salaries paid to its personnel, and its present value and potential worth must be considered. The same economic criteria that are applied to a laboratory or research group may be used for evaluating the center. If its operating costs are excessive when compared with the benefits to be derived from it, other methods must be used to obtain the information.

One way to cut costs may be to search for information less diligently. It may be necessary to furnish less specific information to users to make the service economically justifiable. The information center and the user may agree that a less than completely accurate flow of material will be sufficient to meet the demands of both. The cold reality must be faced that if obtaining information for a particular task costs too much, either the task should be abandoned or it should proceed without the data. When it begins to cost less to conduct an experiment than to find out if the work has already been performed, the information center has become an expensive burden. But the organization that operates on a tight budget, yet anticipates a change in tastes in a marketing area and so allows its company to get there "firstest with the mostest" to meet a new demand and earn a profit, is an indispensable member of the company. However, we must be cautious not to be like the man who, in Oscar Wilde's words, "knows the price of everything and the value of nothing." Improved planning and control and performance follow when a well-informed management keeps up with business and technical events as they happen or are about to happen. This is an important economic advantage to having an information center, and it should not be overlooked.

User orientation. Determining how well the management and technical information center is oriented to the needs of its various users is a frequently overlooked criterion in evaluating the organization's worth. In a sense, this encompasses part of all the other criteria already mentioned. As the center increases in area and scope and is called on to perform additional functions for new communities of users within the company, its staff must guard against neglecting its original clientele. User needs and user satisfaction must be evaluated periodically to insure that changing requirements are considered.

Before organizing the information center, it is advisable to conduct a survey to learn what potential users expect to obtain from it. After it has been in operation for a short period a follow-up survey should be undertaken to determine if users are getting from it what they expect and want and, just as important, what additional services they would like. The user survey will also reveal what segments of the company are not using the services. A study can then be conducted to decide how best to provide the nonusers with information that will assist them in their operations.

This feedback of information as to how well the center is functioning need not wait until a formal survey is made. The number of documents requested from a list of suggested items supplied in response to an inquiry will give an indication of how appropriate the list was. The number of "repeat" users will also attest to how well the information center is fulfilling the needs of its patrons. Services that are proffered but are not being used should be carefully scrutinized; perhaps such services should be discontinued. Establishing and maintaining any management and technical information center service must be predicated on the assumption that the service is fulfilling the needs of the company. A particular service may not be used because (1) personnel do not know it is available, (2) there is no need for it, or (3) it is not fulfilling the need.

In the first instance, the center staff has the responsibility of informing all areas within the company of the existence of the organization and the availability of its services. A tour of the center's facilities should be included as part of the indoctrination of new employees. Bulletin board notices advertising new acquisitions, services, and special activities help educate employees to the benefits that may be derived from the center. One effective method of keeping personnel aware of what is happening in their various fields is to send them reprints of articles and notices of new reports that are applicable to their work. This also encourages members of the organization to take fuller advantage of the services provided by the center.

In the case of services that are no longer needed, they should be discontinued and the money, skills, and time formerly used to maintain them should be applied to areas that are more consistent with the needs of the company. Sometimes a service that should be discontinued is kept up simply because it is in operation. The service may have been useful at one time, but times change, and the information organization with an eye to the future should not hesitate to eliminate an activity which is of no further value.

As to the service that is not fulfilling the need, a good feedback system will indicate whether this is the case. When the services provided are not responsive to the needs of the clients, the administrator of the center should change its modus operandi and make sure these needs are being fulfilled. It is not up to the user to change his requirements; it is up to the center to devise ways of responding positively to these user requirements. One problem may be a failure of communication between the user and the center. The user may phrase his question in such a way that the center employee thinks he is asking for one thing when in fact something else is required. Perspicacious questions by staff members would help clear up such misunderstandings.

User orientation is by far the most critical evaluation criterion for use in determining whether the return on investment from the management and technical information center is worth the expense of maintaining it. If the center meets or exceeds the demands of its users, it has become a profit center as it diverts resources to other areas of company activities.

Which results we get will depend, not so much on our technical competence in linking computers and communications, but on the range and depth of the management judgment we bring to the job. This means to me that the responsibility for managing the information revolution cannot be delegated. Designing a business information system isn't the exclusive province of a specialized department. In the final analysis it is a general management responsibility. And it needs to be a concerted understanding, reflecting a balanced consideration of the needs of the entire organization.

—H. I. ROMNES

X

Automating the Information Center

The automation of a management and technical information center should be carried out in a series of steps that parallel the growth and informational needs of the company it serves. A computerized information organization that provides data for the sole purpose of controlling the inventory of a small corner grocery store or that maintains a manually posted card catalog of parts listings for a popular make of automobile are extreme examples of incompatibility that must be avoided. In the spectrum of information handling which ranges from manual to computer-oriented systems, the basic elements of input, storage and processing, and output are present. Exhibit 20 illustrates this processing flow and shows some of the options that are available in each element.

The *quantity of information needed* will influence the extent to which the center will have to be mechanized. The greater the

amount of material that must be dealt with, the more necessary it is
that the system be automated, everything else being equal. Naturally,
the more extensive the center's storehouse of information, the more
difficult and time consuming it is to locate and retrieve specific items.
Also, increased quantities of information dictate that more space be
provided to store the material, if it is to be retained in its original
form.

Access to the material is another factor that must be weighed
when automation is considered, and the number of users or groups of
users who will have direct contact with the information must be included. In a decentralized corporation whose divisions are separated
geographically but need to exchange basic data, a highly automated
system would be advisable, even necessary. Through a series of
terminals located at the various facilities, each division could insert
data into an information storage bank and withdraw other data as
needed. This material would reflect the inputs of other companies
participating in the system. Such a multi-access feature is frequently
referred to as an "on line" system.

The *speed* with which the information must be provided is a third
element that will affect the degree to which the system becomes
automated. However, as with so many of these factors, promptness is
interrelated with other elements. When dealing with small quantities of information it takes less time to retrieve the needed material
manually than it does to use an automated system. A card can be
withdrawn from a card catalog, a folder from a file, or a report from a
shelf more rapidly than the computer can be queried as to the location of the data. However, when the catalog occupies an entire room
in a building, the files take up an entire floor, and shelves of reports
fill a building, it is obviously more efficient to use some form of
mechanization to locate the data. When information is being continually changed and updated (as with airline reservations or the
tracking of military aircraft and ships) and several different groups
must have access to the latest data, a fully automated information
system is needed. This up-to-the-minute data system is commonly
referred to as "real time."

A fourth factor is the *amount of manipulation and processing and
control* that the data must undergo. The analysis and synthesis of
information can be handled manually, automatically, or in a combination of the two. If the information is basically accounting data,

Exhibit 20. OPTIONS FOR AUTOMATING AN INFORMATION CENTER

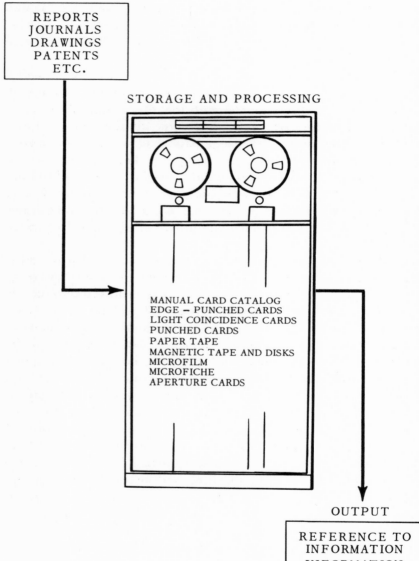

INPUT

REPORTS
JOURNALS
DRAWINGS
PATENTS
ETC.

STORAGE AND PROCESSING

MANUAL CARD CATALOG
EDGE – PUNCHED CARDS
LIGHT COINCIDENCE CARDS
PUNCHED CARDS
PAPER TAPE
MAGNETIC TAPE AND DISKS
MICROFILM
MICROFICHE
APERTURE CARDS

OUTPUT

REFERENCE TO
INFORMATION
INFORMATION
ABSTRACTED
INFORMATION

heavy dependence on automation is in order. If the material consists largely of indexing terms and verbal descriptions to locate facts, these may be translated into numerical equivalents and used in a mechanized system. Many of the operations of an information center are routine or clerical in nature, and these could possibly be handled more efficiently and at less cost by a punched card system than manually. Such operations as preparing renewal notices and lists of holdings, circulation handling, and typing catalog cards lend themselves to mechanization. On the other hand, systems analysis of present operations may indicate that the current methods, with a few manual improvements, may be quite adequate. Just as overdesign sometimes occurs in engineering, the magic of the word "automation" has sometimes resulted in the installation of a computer-based system for an operation whose most sophisticated requirements could be handled by punched cards and dealt with more practically and economically by an efficient clerk.

The *availability of mechanized equipment* in the organization will be a fifth determining factor. Few companies can justify the full-time use of a computer for their information organizations alone. However, if a digital computer is available the possibility of sharing the equipment part of the time certainly exists. Like the other groups in the company, the information center can assume its share of the cost as well as part of the benefit of the computer facility. If the company has EAM (electric accounting machines) equipment as the basis for its data handling, the information center would mechanize through the use of punched cards. If the company subcontracts its data processing to an outside organization, the equipment provided by the vendor will be the limiting factor as to the degree of automation undertaken.

Tools of Information Storage and Retrieval

The *manual card catalog* used in a conventional library is the basis for most information storage and retrieval systems. The user searching for a document that contains an item of desired information looks for it under the subject, the title, or the author's name. Once he locates a card in the catalog listed in one of these three categories, he gives the circulation desk attendant the call number of the document. The clerk retrieves the item from the library shelves. How accurately the material has been cataloged and to what depth it has been indexed when first acquired will determine the ease with which the document is located by the user. Where the information required falls into a combination of several categories, coordinated index searching is not possible because only one card is placed in the index for each subject. For example, if a manager needs information on lasers used to blast holes in Mylar-coated tapes for high-density data storage, he may have to look up each of a number of terms: "lasers," "data storage," "Mylar tapes," and "recording devices." He may find the information he is seeking only after searching various topics. In view of the volume of management and technical information published today, finding a particular straw of fact in the information haystack by manual methods becomes a formidable if not an insurmountable task.

Exhibit 21. EDGE-PUNCHED CARDS

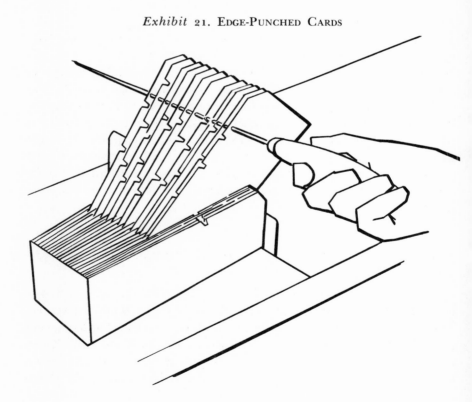

Edge-punched cards offer an inexpensive method of sorting and manipulating small quantities of data mechanically. In such a system, a code is devised to simplify handling. For example, if the system is used to match personnel with job requirements, each job is profiled as to the talents needed to fulfill the openings, and a card is made for each employee. One segment of the card is allocated to represent each of the skills in which the company has an interest. Various holes are punched on the edge of the card, each punch representing a particular skill in which the employee is proficient. When a specific skill is sought, the cards are collected and a needle is inserted through the hole that is applicable to the required skill. A number of cards will fall out of the pile because they are punched or notched at the edge. These cards will bear the names of employees having the particular skills needed. Exhibit 21 illustrates this technique. Variations on this system are available under various trade names, but the basic process-of-elimination principle remains the same.

Optical coincidence cards, sometimes called "peekaboo" cards, provide a practical method of locating information when the number of items or documents in the collection does not exceed 10,000. However, some available systems permit as many as 10 times that number of documents to be searched. The limiting factor is the number of holes that can be punched in the cards. Each item or document in the collection is assigned a number which refers to an identical position on all the cards. A card is made for every term or subject that may conceivably be used in a search for information. All documents coming into the information center are analyzed for the terms that will best describe their contents. These term cards are removed from the files and holes are punched in them, corresponding with the number that has been assigned to the incoming document. The position of the hole that refers to the document is the same on all cards. Thus, if a person is searching for a coordination of terms such as management and information and planning, the term cards referring to each of these subjects are removed from the files and aligned on a light box. Light will pass through the cards for all documents that have been indexed under these terms, thus identifying those particular documents that contain the information needed. The light will not penetrate any other portion of the cards, since the holes will not be aligned. Exhibit 22 illustrates this technique. Unlike manual catalog cards, the optical coincidence method allows for coordination of many indexing terms and provides greater precision in locating material.

The *punched card,* or unit record, has become a standard of record keeping in our daily lives. It appears as checks, bills, time cards, and so on, and usually printed on its face is the admonition, "Do not fold, spindle, or mutilate." The punched card is ideal for storing and handling vast quantities of information from many sources. As in the

Exhibit 22. OPTICAL COINCIDENCE (PEEKABOO) CARDS

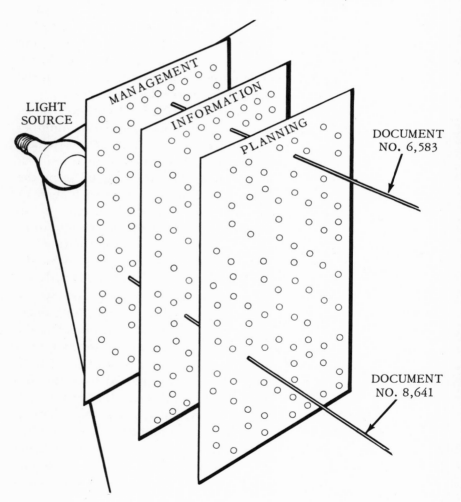

case of optical coincidence cards, all incoming source material is given an identifying number. The information contained in the source document may then be placed in one of several broad categories such as marketing, electronics, or management. The information is further broken down into key words or descriptors used to index the material for later retrieval. These words or terms also have numerical equivalents by which the data can be coded onto the punched cards.

When all pertinent material has been keypunched onto the cards, the cards are verified to insure accuracy in transcribing the material. The next step is to sort the cards into appropriate groupings by document number, category number, or descriptor numbers. After being sorted, the cards can be merged in a collator with already existing cards and filed. When a person asks for specific information, the card sorter is programmed to drop out the cards that match the wanted information. The requester then either receives the information he needs or must reformulate his question to initiate a further search of the files. Exhibit 23 shows a simplified flow chart of a typical punched card system for handling information.

Punched cards are limited to 80 characters on an IBM card or 90 characters on a Remington Rand tabulating card, while *paper tapes* allow a continuous flow of characters to be recorded in a small amount of space. In addition to the document and category numbers and indexing term codes, an abstract or extract of the information may be punched onto the paper tape together with other explanatory data, comments, or references. While the paper tape is being punched, the operator also produces a hard copy of what she is typing. The typed sheet can be used to verify the accuracy of the material; it can also provide a listing of the new information for dissemination. The tape itself is an input or storage device to a computer system, where it can be searched and printed out as needed. In addition, the paper tape may be fed into a special electric typewriter to produce a printout of its contents.

Although paper tapes have proved to be an inexpensive and reliable medium for temporary storage of information, the *magnetic tape* has become the main medium used for storing and processing information on the computer. Large quantities of data can be stored in a very small space on magnetic tape, it can be searched more rapidly, and its printouts are immediately available. Unfortunately, magnetic tape—like paper tape—can be searched only sequentially. To allow random access to huge quantities of information that can be stored in very small areas, *magnetic drums, disks,* and *cards* have been developed.

To cope with vast quantities of information, several microdocumentation techniques have been developed for storing data in minia-

Exhibit 23. FLOW CHART FOR PUNCHED CARD HANDLING OF INFORMATION

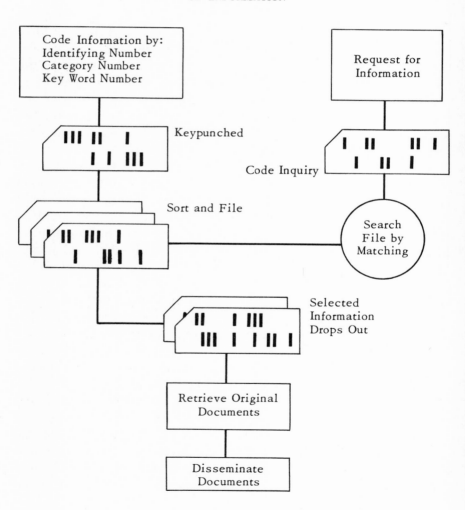

turized formats. Microfilm, film jackets, microfiche, and aperture cards are now standard methods of storing and retrieving information in business, industry, and government as well as in universities and libraries throughout the world. Microimages are helping solve the problem of storage. They have the advantage of preserving the data longer than ordinary paper; they can be viewed and duplicated quickly and economically; and, when combined with data processing techniques, they offer on-the-spot retrieval of original material.

Microfilm is usually 16 mm or 35 mm wide and consists of a continuous roll of film on which has been photographed the information to be stored. The information may consist of bulky maps and engineering drawings, pages of text and illustrations from books and reports, invoices and checks, or whatever. A record is made of the contents of each roll of film; and when someone wishes to view the data, the roll of film is removed from storage, placed in a microfilm viewer, and projected onto a viewing surface. Some viewers also have a printing attachment which permits the viewer to make an on-the-spot copy of the material he wants to study.

Film jackets are strips of 16 mm or 35 mm microfilm placed in a sleeve or jacket of clear acetate. Some of these are attached to card stock and can be edge-punched for later retrieval. In a small business or an area of activity where only a limited amount of documentation is needed, this method provides an adequate means of information storage and retrieval.

Microfiche is a sheet of transparent film containing several microfilm images or "chips." The National Microfilm Association, in conjunction with certain government agencies, has standardized the overall size of the card to 4″ x 6″ and has limited its capacity to no more than 58 page images per card. However, nongovernmental enterprises have found sizes ranging from 3″ x 5″ to 5″ x 8″ more suitable to their needs and have recorded up to 90 frames of information on these sheets.

The aperture card combines the best of both systems. It consists of a standard punched card into which is inserted a microfilmed chip containing from one to eight pages of an image. The aperture card can then be sorted, matched, merged, and so on, the same as any other punched card, and it has the added feature of supplying the actual material for viewing when the punched card is retrieved automatically.

Advances in microform and computer technology and communications, and the relationships of all these, offer disciplines to provide rapid access to information as it develops and also provide a way to store it in compact form. For example, a laser system now on the market can store 44 standard text pages in a space the size of a pinhead. At this rate the entire holdings of the Library of Congress can be stored in four 2,400-foot tape reels. In other systems now available a user simply dials a telephone number, and instantly the document he needs is retrieved from the microfilm storage center. If microwave circuits are used, the subscriber can receive a page every 30 seconds; conventional electronic telephone lines handle only one page every three minutes.

The tools and techniques for managing information are available to the alert businessman who wants to put them to use. But no matter how sophisticated the system decided on, the information it provides can be no better than the information fed into it originally. What is more, the most advanced machines can only provide information upon which decisions can be based. The decisions themselves must be made by competent managers and executives.

THE INFORMATION SYSTEMS SPECIALIST

The information systems specialist is now an integral element of the management and technical information center. In a large group he is usually a full-time staff member. More often he is a member of the electronic data processing group and is consulted when computer programming, flow charting, and similar information handling techniques need to be evaluated or undertaken. But, because the needs of the clients must always be paramount, the manager of the center must not delegate to the systems specialist decisions as to when, if, and how changes to the system are to be made.

Frequently the emerging techniques and changing methods of information handling bring with them a mystical jargon of technology. The information center manager may be overwhelmed and allow the specialist a free rein to decide on changes as long as he remains within budget limitations. Yet the responsibility lies with the manager; he has an obligation to describe clearly to his systems specialist what his problems are and what objectives he hopes to achieve. The specialist may make alternate proposals on how those goals may best be accomplished within the current state of the art, taking into consideration such parameters as personnel and budget. However, the ultimate decision must be made by the manager of the information organization, who alone fully realizes the ramifications of all changes and how they will help—or hinder—the functioning of the center.

> The distinction between the control system of the plant . . . and the ADP system of the office will disappear. One information system will feed the entire business. This system will be the arteries through which flow the life stream of the business: market intelligence, control information, strategy decisions, feedback for change.
>
> —JOHN DIEBOLD

XI

The Sigma Approach

The typical company that has been in existence for a number of years has established various sources of information within its own area. In the early stages the information flow is informal, usually oral in nature. As the company expands, the areas where information is collected usually fall into departmental lines: financial data from the finance group, manpower information from the personnel office, technical information from the research and development department, marketing information from the sales division.

It soon becomes apparent to management that, when decisions are made relating to these various departments, consideration must be given to other aspects of the company and to additional information received from outside the organization. If the firm has its own data processing equipment or has access to EAM or EDP facilities, it is feasible and logical to have a total information system installed. This is the pattern of present thinking, as is evident in the national scene where elements of the Federal Government have recommended establishment of a national data center, a centralized depository for all statistical facts collected about an individual by various government agencies. These individual statistics would be stored by EDP methods and retrieved as needed.

The concept of such a monolithic apparatus has aroused fears of the invasion of personal privacy or violation of confidential documents in the citizens of the United States. The same fears have been expressed by department managers of organizations considering the "total system" concept. The sigma approach eliminates this fear.

Basically, the sigma system is a switching system or clearinghouse concept. It permits data to be gathered, analyzed, stored, and retrieved in the specialized areas of operation in a company and yet allows the other groups to benefit from these storehouses of information. The sigma concept is based on a free flow of information from and to all areas.

Most proposals for integrated information systems or total systems are based on the assumption that the company has access to computer facilities and that many housekeeping functions can be handled more efficiently by electronic data processing. The heavy concentration is on automating such activities as inventory control, payroll, purchasing, and billing. In most instances the results show a better performance of these tasks; but there is also an increased generation of information from the computer printers. Automation may actually compound a company's information problem with the additional printouts of data. What management needs is not additional proliferation of information but assimilation of information.

Exhibit 24 is a typical organization chart. Each block represents a major division within the company structure; each also symbolizes a major source of information. Much of the data generated by each division is used solely within that division. However, the people in each block need a certain amount of information that is forthcoming from other divisions. Besides this intracompany need for information, there is a requirement for data that can be obtained only from outside the organization. This externally generated material is usually gathered independently by each division, although in many instances the same information is needed by several divisions.

Top management in this typical company would have to consult with representatives from each of these divisions, if information were needed. Before the information could be used, executive management would probably have to summarize it and combine it with the details received from each of the divisions. Finally, the facts gleaned

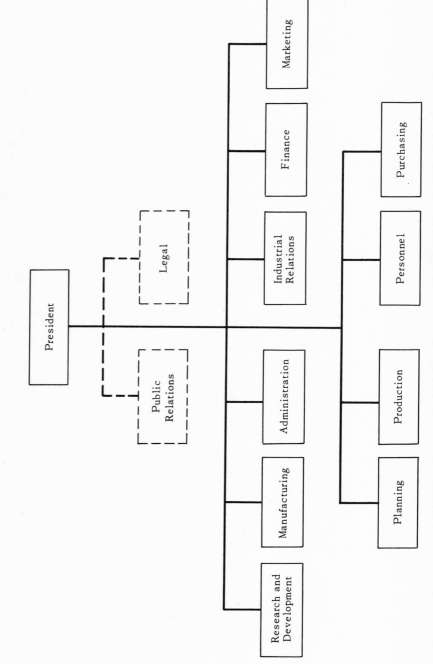

Exhibit 24. TYPICAL COMPANY ORGANIZATION CHART

from outside the company would have to be factored into the gathered data before meaningful decisions could be made.

The sigma approach to management and technical information would eliminate duplication of information gathering, relieve top management of the work of preliminary analysis and synthesis, and increase the flow of information within the company. Exhibit 25 shows how the information center would operate within the typical organizational structure shown in Exhibit 24.

Since the sigma method allows for semiautonomous information depots to continue operating within the company structure, few divisions will resist its introduction. The usual traumas that accompany a change in the mode of operation are avoided when this system is adopted. There is no threat of job elimination. As a matter of fact, it assures the existing information gathering group of continued work. The individual's fear of needing to orient himself abruptly to a new method of doing his job does not apply. Sometimes, the only major change may be that summaries of existing reports have to be prepared and turned over to the information center.

The detailed information needed by operating personnel in the conduct of their jobs will still be handled within the respective departments. Through a series of remote terminals, divisions which need computerized arithmetic and logic will have on-line, real-time, and time-sharing use of the computer facilities to prepare their daily reports and process operating data such as billings, purchasing, and inventory control. However, minor and major summaries of each division's activities, prepared by the originating division, will be submitted to the management and technical information center at scheduled intervals.

Subject specialists at the center will analyze and synthesize these activity summaries, evaluate them against the planned activities, and supply management with the information in a meaningful format. In addition, the center will receive all reports, documents, and other data prepared in the company. Subject specialists will classify, index, cross-reference, and summarize this material by subject, title, author, contract, and other categories by which it may later be retrieved. All externally generated material requested by personnel in various divisions will be handled through the information center. There the data will be analyzed before being delivered to the user. In addition, the center will continually acquire data from external sources in

Exhibit 25. SIGMA APPROACH

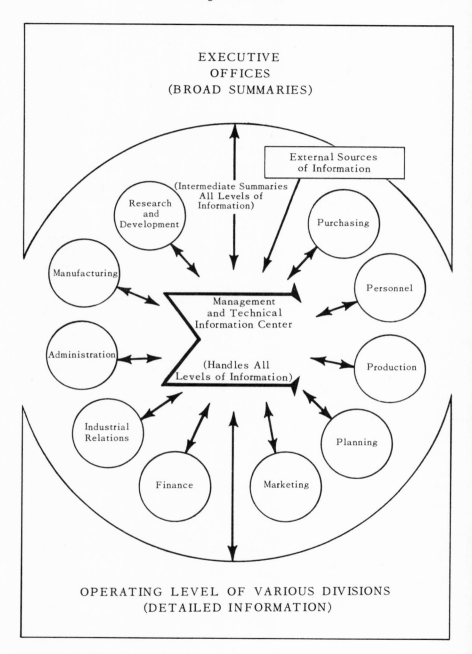

anticipation of needs, as well as to fulfill requests for information.

Sensitive information—proprietary data originating in the research and development divisions, cost data prepared in the finance division for proposals still being bid, industrial relations material such as personnel data and labor relations plans during contract negotiation —will be handled so that only individuals having a need to know, as stipulated by the originating division, will have access to the data. Similarly, information regarding national security will be handled with all the precautions demanded by industrial and federal security requirements. Thus safeguards will be built into the system to limit accessibility to information when it is necessary to do so.

From a mathematical standpoint, the sigma approach can be described as a summation of all the internal and external information that is germane to the company's activities. Each information-creating group within the company assembles its own data, facts, and reports into meaningful formats for its own use, cumulates this material for use by its own management, and turns a summary over to the information center. Meanwhile, the information organization has provided data received from external sources to the various groups on demand or in anticipation of need and also has transferred information among a multitude of groups within the company. An integration of the various summaries is then made at the information center; the total summary is made available to top-level management to help provide a clear-cut, broad view of the company's activities. The concept can be expressed in this formula:

$$\sum \begin{matrix}\text{Sigma}\\\text{System}\end{matrix} = \sum\begin{matrix}\text{External}\\\text{Information}\end{matrix} + \sum\begin{matrix}\text{R\&D}\\\text{Info}\end{matrix} + \sum\begin{matrix}\text{Mfg.}\\\text{Info}\end{matrix} + \sum\begin{matrix}\text{Sales}\\\text{Info}\end{matrix} + \cdots \sum\begin{matrix}\text{Other}\\\text{Company}\\\text{Info}\end{matrix}$$

The philosophy of the sigma approach is that all levels of management are kept informed so as to make them better able to meet their scheduled commitments, operate within their cost goals, develop new business, and maintain technical competence by keeping current with new advances in the state of the art.

Each element within the company makes a complete plan for each of its tasks. This plan is subdivided into controllable elements, and the various levels of supervision are informed as to what segments of the plan they are responsible for implementing. With a clearly

Exhibit 26. PERT Network

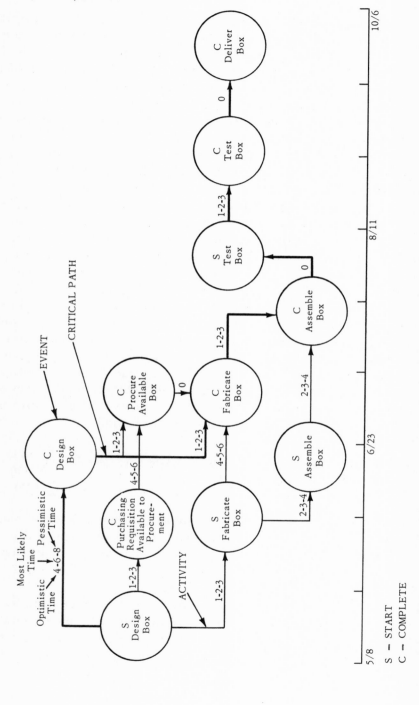

S – START
C – COMPLETE

defined and easily comprehended plan, about 75 percent of all problems can be solved by first-level supervision with daily follow-up and expediting. Using this management-by-exception technique, middle management would account for the solution of 15 percent of the problems. The remaining 10 percent of the problems are taken to top management for final resolution. Thus top management is relieved of unnecessary details and still has the tools to forecast new business opportunities and avert problems before they occur.

The information center possesses summaries of these task plans which contain—

- What is to be done (scope of work) .
- When it is to be accomplished (time schedule) .
- How it is to be executed (functional work flow) .
- Who is to do the work (manpower plan) .
- Where it will be implemented (facilities plan) .
- Why it will be profitable (budget control plan) .

Details of the various plans are retained in the separate groups responsible for their fulfillment. Thus all elements of the company are alerted to their individual responsibilities to adhere to technical performance, time schedules, and cost controls.

One of the tools that the information center should use if it has access to computer facilities is PERT (Program Evaluation and Review Technique) . PERT is not management by computer. It does not solve problems, but it does display them in perspective so that all related factors can be judged. The PERT technique provides a logical, time-phased plan to achieve a stated goal or objective; it enables more efficient use of available resources and reveals the probability of meeting required objective dates.

PERT employs a network (Exhibit 26) which is a graphic representation of a plan. The PERT chart displays the sequence and interrelationships of tasks needed to reach a specific, definable objective. The network consists of events. An event is a zero point in time that represents an accomplishment, a decision point, or a milestone. The connecting link between events requires time and is called an activity. An activity is work in process, resources being consumed, and man-hours being expended.

Three time estimates are used for each activity. These are statistically averaged and ultimately used in calculations to determine the duration of the project and the probability of meeting the required objective date. "Optimistic time" estimates are the minimum time required if everything goes without a hitch. "Most likely" reflects time that will occur most often in normal circumstances. "Pessimistic" is the longest time an activity will take if everything goes wrong.

The critical path is the sequence of activities and events that requires the optimum time. It is also the path with the least amount of slack. "Slack time" is the difference between the time it is expected to take to complete the project and the time within which it is scheduled to be completed. "Slack" may be positive where there is more than ample time to complete the job. "Zero slack" indicates an on-schedule condition, while "negative slack" reveals a behind-schedule situation. The activities along this critical path are closely monitored for necessary corrective action.

With PERT and other management planning and control techniques, such as line-of-balance charts for production planning, the information center would receive and retain graphic displays and summary reports necessary to maintain a consolidated overall picture of the company, including—

- A master plan, upon which are scheduled the significant events that must be accomplished.
- A work breakdown structure, which defines the tasks to be performed and their relationship to the end item.
- Detailed PERT networks for first-level management, which represent an integration of the various elements of the work breakdown structure. Constant analysis of earliest completion dates versus slack time available will allow supervisors to make adjustments in time to meet schedules.
- Summary PERT networks for top and middle management, which are condensations of the detailed networks. Key milestones and other salient items with which top management is concerned are graphically displayed on these summary networks.
- PERT/Time reports, which list events, scheduled completion dates, and slack time within which the task must be completed. Top management can use this report to review events which either pace the program or show much positive slack time. The pacing events represent the critical path and must be met on time for successful completion of the program on schedule. Ex-

cessive positive slack indicates too much time and resources are being allowed and alerts management to the need to determine whether the surplus resources could be diverted effectively to more critical areas.

• PERT/Cost summary reports, which will allow management to trace quickly the source of a potential cost deviation at any level of the work breakdown structure and to institute corrective action.

• Manpower control reports, which permit management to compare the allocation of a type of labor being expended concurrently on various tasks. This allows top management to reallocate manpower from a noncritical area to one that may be behind schedule.

• Technical summary progress reports, which highlight any tech-

Exhibit 27. SIGMA CAPSULE

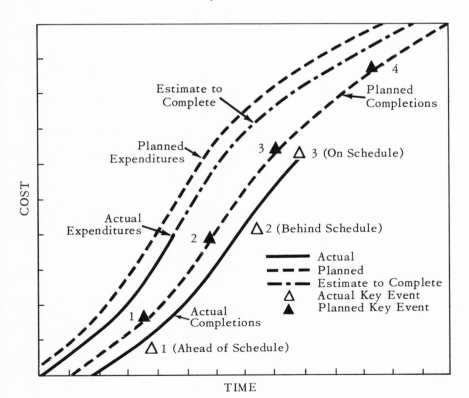

nical problems that must be resolved. Top management's scrutiny of these reports reveals what areas of the company are technically weak and where technical competence must be improved.

Such summing up of activities keeps schedule, technical, and financial areas under constant, meaningful surveillance so that remedial measures may be undertaken before a problem rages out of control. The capsule information available to top management from the information center would spotlight problems, show progress, and indicate successful completion of business activities as well as predict trends and emphasize the need for corrective action. Exhibit 27 is a typical capsule summary that the information organization would supply to top management.

The sigma approach thus provides for both vertical and horizontal access to information. Broad directive policies and queries flow downward through the various levels of management, as reports and information flow upward in compliance with policy and in answer to questions. By the same token, all operating divisions of the company share the same data base upon which to make decisions. All members are aware of what is occurring in other divisions which may affect them or on which they may have an effect. Unlike a monolithic total information system, allowing for no individual participation of data handling, the sigma information system acts as a vehicle for transferring information; it performs a summarizing function for management, stating what the company has done, what it is doing, and what it should be doing in the light of current events. All areas of the company contribute to its function and all benefit from its services.

We are learning how to take the information that controls the world and put it in such standard language as to make possible its gathering, dissemination, processing, and utilization on a scale that uplifts the total brainpower of the world, on the one hand, and reduces most of what is needed to operate the world, on the other hand, to a common language that will cross national and racial and conventional language barriers.

—SIMON RAMO

XII

National and International Information Networks

In addition to the information generated from within a company, vast quantities of management and technical data are available from trade associations, schools and universities, the trade press, and the government.

In the field of management information, the American Management Association is unique in that its major reasons for existence are to find, develop, and share better skills and techniques of management. It sponsors courses and meetings and provides information and publication services covering the complete spectrum of management responsibilities. It keeps members informed of new techniques and procedures that they may apply to their own special situations. Other professional organizations also publish information on the latest trends in specific areas of management and conduct conferences and seminars for the exchange of ideas in their particular fields. Active support of these associations not only benefits the respective societies, but—more important—alerts management to the current developments in the areas of interest.

Just as management has its professional societies, so do the various scientific and technical disciplines. Throughout the year these professional associations publish journals and reports containing the latest information about their fields of interest; they hold regular meetings where their members exchange ideas and discuss new developments. Because so many of the fields of science and engineering cross disciplines, several of these societies have banded together for mutual information sharing. For example, the Engineering Societies Library of the United Engineering Trustees numbers a dozen founder and associate societies. By adopting this approach to a national interchange of engineering data, the Engineering Societies Library has become the largest engineering library in the free world. It boasts a collection of 190,000 volumes on the level of the graduate and practicing engineer and receives more than 3,500 periodicals from some 50 countries in 25 languages. The *Engineering Index,* which averages about 45,000 annotated references annually, is based on publications received by the Engineering Societies Library.

NATIONAL INFORMATION NETWORK

The Federal Government, in conjunction with elements of industry which are interested in voluntarily coordinating information handling within the limits of competition, proprietary information, and security, has begun the task of investigating and implementing a national information network. In the Federal budget for 1967, more than $15.5 billion has been allocated for research and development. The scientific and technical information returned from such investment is a national resource that must not be lost in a paper jungle. To control this flood of information so that public and private enterprise benefit equally, $400 million was spent in fiscal 1966 for scientific and technical information activities.

Federal concern with the information problem is not new. In the past ten years, more than a dozen reports have come from Senate and House committees (as well as recommendations from private groups) suggesting ways in which scientific and technical information may be made more readily available within Government agencies and among private businesses. In the tradition of free enterprise the emphasis, naturally, has been on keeping Federal intervention and centralization to a minimum. As Vice President Humphrey stated (when he was chairman of the Senate Subcommittee on Reorganization and International Organization),

> Better handling of pre-publication information is essential, although, in the final analysis, it is the control of post-publication data, i.e., on the final results of experiments, which is the most important challenge. Thus there must be a clear, strong top policy mandate for effective and efficient management of pre-publication and post-publication information. . . . The mandate should be implemented in a manner consistent with the private enterprise and decentralized character of American industry, university, and other effort. A monolithic information complex is neither feasible nor desirable; a flexible, interlocking network, based on voluntary agreement, is desirable.[7]

President Kennedy's Science Advisory Committee, headed by Dr. Alvin M. Weinberg, amplified the idea further in suggesting:

> We believe that the specialized information center, backed by large central depositories, might well become a dominant means for transfer of technical information. . . . A specialized information center makes it its business to know everything that is being published in a special field, such as nuclear spectroscopy or the thermophysical properties of chemical compounds; it collates and reviews the data, and provides its subscribers with regularly issued compilations, critical reviews, specialized bibliographies, and other such tools. . . . Since the technical information center in this sense must be part of science and technology, it is natural that it be located where relevant science is flourishing. The Panel therefore urges that new information centers be established at public and private technical institutions, not as adjuncts of general libraries or of publishing ventures, or of central depositories. Where research and development is done for the government at government laboratories, national laboratories, universities, or industrial laboratories, information centers in related fields ought to find a congenial atmosphere.[8]

In the closing paragraphs of its report the committee warns,

> We must always seek to insure, on behalf of both the Federal Gov-

ernment and the technical community, that the federal information system remains adequate but does not overwhelm the existing non-government systems, and that our government and non-government systems continue to develop into an effectively interwoven instrument that is always responsive to the changing needs of our science and technology.[9]

One of the basic recommendations made by President Johnson's Committee on Scientific and Technical Information (COSATI) is that the Federal Government has the responsibility to insure that there exists within the United States at least one accessible copy of each significant publication of the worldwide scientific and technical literature. The responsibility, not necessarily the operation, of an information handling system by the Government is what is stressed in this 1965 report.

Many of these recommendations and suggestions have been put into practice already, to the benefit of both industry and government. The United States is well on its way toward the accomplishment of a voluntary national information network. The forward-looking company which plans to establish a management and technical information center compatible with this system will be among the first to reap the profits of such a network. Even now, companies may avail themselves of the wealth of information that is there for the asking.

The *Government Printing Office* publishes and sells material prepared by the Congress and other governmental agencies. Excellent marketing data gathered by the Department of Commerce can be obtained through the GPO. Small Business Administration publications to aid the man just starting his own business or the established businessman confronting a new problem are for sale by the GPO. Also published by the agency are bulletins on such topics as employee earnings and hours in various retail trades, as assembled by the U.S. Department of Labor. In technical areas, publications range from an industrial plant equipment handbook to a symposium on passive gravity-gradient stabilization. GPO publishes a *Monthly Catalog of United States Government Publications,* which lists by agency what it has printed or is in the process of printing. In addition, it issues a free bi-weekly list of *Selected United States Government Publications* with annotations and prices.

The *Clearinghouse for Federal Scientific and Technical Informa-*

tion (CFSTI) is a part of the Institute for Applied Technology, an agency of the Department of Commerce. Its nearly 300 employees have a budget of more than $5 million with which to answer and redistribute reports prepared by and for more than 30 Federal agencies, including unclassified material from the Department of Defense, National Aeronautics and Space Administration, and Atomic Energy Commission. CFSTI is ready to help industry, for, as stated in its charter, "its purpose is to establish and maintain . . . a clearinghouse for the collection and dissemination of scientific, technical, and engineering information, and to this end to take such steps . . . to make such information available to industry and business, to state and local governments, to other agencies of the Federal Government, and to the general public."

In line with these responsibilities, CFSTI publishes a semimonthly *Government-wide Index to Federal Research and Development Reports.* This is a single reference guide to new, unclassified Government-sponsored research and development of the physical sciences, engineering, and related technology. This index is compiled from all the current announcement journals of the Atomic Energy Commission, National Aeronautics and Space Administration, Defense Documentation Center, and the Clearinghouse itself. A listing of current research and development projects and abstracts of such reports appears in its *U.S. Government Research and Development Reports,* published twice monthly.

In cooperation with the Special Libraries Association Translations Center and the European Translations Centre, *Technical Translations* is issued semimonthly to announce to the public the availability and order information for translated scientific and technical reports, periodicals, and books. Scientific abstracts from Communist countries are available to industry from CFSTI under such titles as *USSR Abstracts* and *East European Scientific Abstracts.* Journals available by subscription are *Communist Chinese Scientific Abstracts* and *Soviet-Bloc Research in Geophysics, Astronomy and Space.*

Research review packages prepared especially for industry are published under the series title *A Review of Selected U.S. Government Research and Development Reports.* The series combines résumés, abstracts, and bibliographies on subject areas (flame-retardant textiles, for example) which offer ideas on material and product development and on means of reducing costs.

The Defense Documentation Center (DDC) is the central facility of the *Department of Defense* for the secondary distribution of technical research and development reports. DDC's services are free to Government agencies, their contractors, subcontractors, and grantees, as well as to potential Department of Defense contractors.

Twice a month, DDC publishes the *Technical Abstract Bulletin* in which it announces and describes to its users its latest acquisitions. The *Technical Abstract Bulletin* records about 60,000 reports annually. Its staff also makes free bibliographic searches on request and provides technical documents in full size or microfiche to qualified users.

Dr. Robert B. Stegmaier, Jr., DDC administrator, states, "Using DDC products, a researcher can save his organization thousands or even millions of dollars by determining quickly whether all or part of a particular project has already been accomplished by another research group. Or, if he determines that his project is not being duplicated, he may learn about various recorded experiments and experiences that will serve as valuable time-saving guides."

With more than 500 operating personnel and an annual budget of approximately $11.5 million, DDC's services should be used by the aggressive firm which wants to take advantage of up-to-date material on information being uncovered by Department of Defense agencies and which is qualified to receive the data.

The Department of Defense also sponsors approximately 300 information analysis centers where data are evaluated and state-of-the-art reports are published in specific areas of activity. The Thermophysical Properties Research Center at Purdue University, The Shock and Vibration Information Center at the Naval Research Laboratory in Washington, and the Human Engineering Information and Analysis Service at Tufts University are examples of the scope of these activities. Reports produced by these centers are available through the DDC distribution organization.

The *National Aeronautics and Space Administration* (NASA), like the Department of Defense, also sponsors information analysis centers and publishes semimonthly an abstracting and indexing journal, *Scientific and Technical Aerospace Reports* (STAR). With NASA's collection of aerospace documents growing at the rate of 75,000 titles annually, STAR affords a comprehensive coverage of worldwide report literature on the science and technology of space and aeronautics. By special arrangement between NASA and the American Institute of Aeronautics and Astronautics, the latter's publication *International Aerospace Abstracts* (IAA) is issued in coordination with STAR. IAA provides worldwide coverage of scientific and technical journals, books, and symposium papers.

NASA issues a series of publications reporting technical innovations that have potential value for industry as a whole. These bulletins are of special interest to companies in fields other than aerospace. The reports range from one- or two-page bulletins to technology surveys that are actually comprehensive state-of-the-art summaries of advances in a complete field. NASA's Office of Technology Utilization is another agency through which business and industry may gain access to NASA's storehouse of information. Through regional dissemination centers that offer (1) selective dissemination, (2) retrospective searches, and (3) publications distribution, NASA is trying to move fresh and useful concepts as well as new materials and processes into fields other than those in which they were originated. Thus NASA is fulfilling the dicta of its enabling legislation of 1958 that "the aeronautical and space activities of the United States shall be conducted so as to contribute . . . to the expansion of human knowledge of phenomena in the atmosphere and space. The administration shall provide for the widest practicable and appropriate dissemination of information concerning its activities and the results thereof."

Since 1947, the *Atomic Energy Commission* has been publishing *Nuclear Science Abstracts*. These include abstracts of reports, books, patents, and journal literature on nuclear science and technology published throughout the world. The Atomic Energy Commission also publishes the following review journals which have application outside Government operations: *Nuclear Safety, Power Reactor Technology, Nuclear Materials, Reactor Fuel Processing,* and *Isotopes and Radiation Technology.*

The Science Information Exchange of the *Smithsonian Institution* provides private management and Government administrators with literature related to current technical research. Financed by the National Science Foundation, the Science Information Exchange keeps abreast of research projects taking place in public and private institutions in the United States as well as overseas, and so, in effect, forewarns against needless duplication of effort during a research project. A *Notice of Research Project* containing a 200-word technical summary of each task contains the highlights of the unpublished research—who is working on it, where it is being conducted, and so on.

The *National Referral Center for Science and Technology,* an arm of the Library of Congress, has a goal of establishing the most direct contact possible between people looking for information and those who can provide it. Unlike a reference activity, which would cite books, journals, and other bibliographic sources, the primary function of the center is to refer its clients to people who can assist them and advise where the information is to be found. In conjunction with these aims, the center also publishes directories of information sources in particular fields of science and technology.

INTERNATIONAL INFORMATION NETWORKS

In spite of the many political and diplomatic barriers that have been erected among nations in the past two decades, the flow of theoretical and pure science information on an international basis is continuous, and the quality of information is excellent. Naturally, each nation guards its military (applied and theoretical) technical knowledge with the utmost care. However, the United Nations Educational, Scientific, and Cultural Organization (UNESCO) has contributed significantly to the growth of information centers in various parts of the world. The 1963 *Guide to the World's Abstracting and Indexing Services in Science and Technology* listed 1,955 titles of articles published in 40 nations. Although the United States, Germany, Japan, France, and the USSR account for more than 50 percent of these titles, nearly 1,000 were spread among the other 35 countries.

The International Exchange Service of the Smithsonian Institution is the main agency through which the United States exchanges reports with other nations. In accordance with agreements, the Exchange Service mails documents originated in the United States to foreign countries and receives from these nations similar technical journals and reports which are then distributed among various governmental agencies.

About 60 percent of the world's technical journals are printed in English, with Russian, German, French, Japanese, and Spanish accounting for another 35 percent. As mentioned earlier, a major effort is being made to translate these foreign documents into English so that the American people may benefit from the technological advances being achieved in foreign countries. More than $3 million is being spent each year in the United States alone to have translations made of nonclassified material.

For example, late in 1966 a team of Communist Chinese chemists were able to synthesize the complex insulin molecule, one of the major chemicals of human life. Although most Americans were surprised and perhaps dubious about the authenticity of the announcement originating in Mao's China, Western biochemists were fully cognizant of the years of work which preceded the disclosure. Reports in *Scientia Sinica,* published in English by the Chinese Academy of Science and available in the United States, had revealed the details about the synthesis of insulin.

Russia, too, has encountered the problem of the information explosion. In 1952 it established Vseseyusnyy Institut Nauchney i Teknicheskey Informatsii (VINITI), the All-Union Institute for Scientific and Technological Information. VINITI receives scientific and technical information from nearly 100 countries in more than 50 languages. From the 12,000 foreign and 2,500 domestic journals reviewed in VINITI, it publishes each month the *Referativny Zhurnal* (Abstract Journal), containing nearly a million abstracts annually.

In addition to the abstract journal, VINITI issues *Ekspress Informatsiya* (Express Information) for important abstracts that need to be circulated quickly. An item appearing in this rapid-dissemination bulletin is in print no more than four to six weeks after the item was originally published. Retrospective searches resulting in state-of-the-art reports are published in *Itegi Nauki* (Scientific Results).

France, like Russia, has a centralized operation for keeping people abreast of current scientific and technical breakthroughs. Through its Centre National de la Recherche Scientifique, it publishes the *Bulletin Signalétique* (Descriptive Report), an abstracting and indexing journal covering nearly 400,000 articles each year.

The idea that valuable scientific information crosses international boundaries only in diplomatic pouches or in the brains of defectors has no real basis in truth. More and more, as nations throughout the world concentrate on establishing their own information networks, it becomes apparent that the day is not too far distant when international information networks will become a reality. The company which has already initiated an information system will be the first to reap the benefits of these national and international approaches to information transfer.

One of the major opportunities for en-
hancing the effectiveness of our national
scientific and technical effort and the ef-
ficiency of Government management of research and development lies in the improvement of our ability to communicate information about current research efforts and the
results of past efforts. . . . Strong science
and technology is a national necessity, and
adequate communication is a prerequisite
for strong science and technology.

—JOHN F. KENNEDY

XIII

Postscript

With the proliferation of technical, management, and industrial information, management and technical information centers in industry have come into being as a natural outgrowth of special or company libraries. The analyzed and synthesized information
disseminated from the center in many cases earns more for the company than it costs to operate the center.

The information center offers immediate value to management.
Savings made in preventing duplicate research efforts, more economical utilization of professional talent, and ready access to information for management decision making are only a few of the advantages gained in establishing such a center.

How valuable an efficient information center can be is reflected in
this description of what happens when a less than professional handling of information takes place within a company. "The director of
an engineering organization spent $50,000 and a year's time in re-
peating an unsuccessful design program for building military trucks.
He had rejected it himself ten years earlier, but he couldn't profit by

his experience because the original report was buried in the company library." [10]

The benefits of the information center to the company in planning are manifold. With new fields opening in science and technology continually, new markets and new products are developing daily. Yesterday's glamour industries are being supplanted by today's dreams transformed into tomorrow's realities. Blue-sky thinking is usually recorded in the scientific management periodicals and journals received in the information center. The responsible information center director alerts the management of his company to these potential profit areas, so long-range planning can reflect such ideas. The center also assists in near-term planning, presenting to management news of the changing needs of customers and the emergence of competitive products. For example, a company manufacturing a silicon-controlled rectifier saved a minimum of two months of research and several thousand dollars by making timely use of information gleaned from a NASA document. The report showed various means of changing the turn-off time of silicon-controlled rectifiers. Using these facts, after two days of testing the company extended the frequency range of its own rectifier.

Tied in closely with the planning values of the information center are its important growth values. The wealth of meaningful data accumulated over the years acts as building blocks for the company's expansion. Synthesizing the varied facts received from many sources sparks new ideas from which management may profit. Also, a search through the backlog of stored information may warn of known or potential pitfalls that management should avoid. The information center acts as a company's bank of information, storing facts that pay good dividends over a period of time.

With the crisis in information reaching national and international proportions, the potential values of the information center become readily apparent. The Government has recognized its responsibilities to transfer information from authors to users and is currently in the process of evaluating and trying out the various methods of accomplishing this task. The company which has already in existence an information center can quickly profit from this developing national information network.

But good technical and management information is no cure-all for bad management. Bad information always leads to bad management, but good information does not of itself insure good management. Information is only one of the tools of management. The ability to put the information to work is what determines the successful manager. Therefore, when skilled management is supplied with good information, the results will prove that the information center is indeed management's hidden asset.

Notes

Foreword: Jay W. Forrester, professor of industrial management, Massachusetts Institute of Technology, in Martin Greenberger, editor, *Management and the Computer of the Future,* John Wiley & Sons, Inc., New York, 1962, p. 37.

   I: General Howell M. Estes, commander of the Military Airlift Command, in "Will Managers Be Overwhelmed by the Information Explosion?" Armed Forces Management, December 1966, p. 84.

  II: Peter F. Drucker, professor of management, New York University, and management consultant, in *Managing for Results,* Harper & Row, Publishers, Inc., New York, 1964, p. 5.

 III: Lyndon B. Johnson, in *The Federal Paperwork Jungle,* 89th Congress, Washington, D.C., February 18, 1965, p. 76.

  IV: W. A. Pulver, president, Lockheed-Georgia, in "Computer System Helps Managers Subdue Giant," *Steel,* January 30, 1967, p. 49.

   V: Hubert H. Humphrey, in *Coordination of Information on Current Federal Research and Development Projects in the Field of Electronics,* 87th Congress, Washington, D.C., September 20, 1961, p. vii.

  VI: Henry Blackstone, president, Servo Corporation of America, quoted in H. B. Maynard, *Top Management Handbook,* McGraw-Hill Book Company, Inc., New York, 1960, p. 201.

 VII: Rear Admiral Thomas J. Rudden, Jr., U.S.N., Deputy Chief of Naval Material, in "Management Information Systems: The Lifeblood of Management," *Defense Industry Bulletin,* January 1967, p. 12.

VIII: J. Paul Getty, in *How to Be Rich,* Playboy Press, Chicago, 1965, p. 84. Copyright © 1961 by HMH Publishing Company, Inc.

  IX: *Science, Government, and Information,* a Report of the President's Science Advisory Committee, January 10, 1963, pp. 10–11.

   X: H. I. Romnes, chairman of the board, American Telephone and Telegraph Company, in "Managing the Information Revolution," *Signal,* October 1966, p. 23.

XI: John Diebold, president and founder of the Diebold Group, Inc., in "ADP—The Still-Sleeping Giant," *Harvard Business Review,* September–October 1964, p. 64.

XII: Simon Ramo, vice chairman and director, TRW Inc., in "Science Turns to Challenge of Satisfying Human Needs," *Technology Week,* January 23, 1967, p. 78.

XIII: John F. Kennedy, in *Science, Government, and Information,* a Report of the President's Science Advisory Committee, January 10, 1963, p. iii.

FOOTNOTES

1. "Inform for Profit Growth," *Steel,* August 28, 1961, p. 51.
2. Francis Bello, "How to Cope with Information," *Fortune,* September 1960, p. 162.
3. "Objectives and Standards for Special Libraries," *Special Libraries,* December 1964, p. 672.
4. Joseph C. Shipman, "Bibliographic Organization in the Physical Sciences," *Wilson Library Bulletin,* April 1966, p. 707.
5. Francis Bello, *op. cit.,* p. 163.
6. U.S. Congress, Senate, Committee on Government Operations, *Coordination of Information on Current Federal Research and Development Projects in the Field of Electronics,* 87th Congress, Washington, D.C., September 20, 1961, p. xxx.
7. *Ibid.*
8. *Science, Government, and Information,* a Report of the President's Science Advisory Committee, January 10, 1963, pp. 32–33.
9. *Ibid.,* p. 51.
10. "Inform for Profit Growth," *Steel,* August 28, 1961, pp. 50–51.

Glossary

abstract—a short summary of a document.

abstract, descriptive—describes the scope of the material generally but does not summarize the contents.

abstract, informative—contains the conclusions formed in the original document and any other significant facts to make the abstract comprehensive.

abstract services—announcement devices such as journals or packets of cards which contain abstracts of recently published articles along with bibliographical data to aid the researcher in obtaining the original source material.

access—the means by which information is reached in an information system.

access, random—direct locating of stored information without recourse to other material stored in the system.

access, sequential—locating of stored information through a specific sequence in order to obtain the information needed.

acquisition—the obtaining of informational material for current or future needs.

active reference service—an information center service consisting of performing reference work for the user and supplying him with the results of the investigation.

activity—in PERT, the connecting link between events which require time, such as work in process, resources being consumed, man-hours being expended.

ADP—automatic data processing.

annotation—critical description or evaluation of the contents or material.

aperture card—a tabulated or punched card with an open space provided for mounting a piece of microfilm.

batch processing—a grouping together of similar items for machine processing at the same time, as opposed to on-line processing.

bibliography—a list of references to information that is pertinent to a particular subject.

bibliography, annotated—a bibliography which contains comments on the various items listed.

Brussels classification. See **universal decimal classification.**

catalog—a listing of the holdings of an information center containing sufficient descriptions to locate the items. In a card catalog each item is recorded on a separate card and indexed by such terms as subject, author, and title.

category—a natural grouping of related material.

CFSTI—Clearinghouse for Federal Scientific and Technical Information.

classifying—the assigning of informational material into related categories.

clearinghouse—a single location from which information that originated in more than one place is distributed.

collection—the total information resources available to the users of the information center.

comprehensive search—a search of current and past information that covers all the material available on a particular subject within the constraints of time and money.

coordinate indexing—an indexing method by which information is located by the manipulation of two or more indexing terms.

COSATI—Committee on Scientific and Technical Information.

critical path—in PERT, the optimum sequence of activities and events that require the optimum time with the least amount of slack.

current awareness—the system by which the announcement of newly published information is brought to the attention of individuals whose fields of interest coincide with the material.

current awareness search—a search of the unpublished and recently published material covering a specific area of interest.

data processing—the mechanical manipulation of quantitative material such as payrolls and inventories to decrease the space occupied by each individual item of information and increase the speed by which it is handled.

DDC—Defense Documentation Center.

degree of risk—the amount of chance a person is willing to take in making a wrong decision; it is inversely proportional to the quantity of information available. Also referred to as **probability of error.**

descriptor—a word or combination of words used to describe a concept in a document or other information material.

Dewey decimal classification—a classification system for books and other documents whereby all knowledge is divided into ten main classes, each designated by a three-digit number; subdivisions are noted by numbers following a decimal point.

documentation—the preparation, handling, and distribution of informational material.

EAM—electric accounting machine, used for processing punched cards.

edge-punched cards—cards notched on their edges to encode data for later retrieval.

EDP—electronic data processing, using computers for processing information.

event—in PERT, a zero point in time that represents an accomplishment, a decision point, or a milestone.

exhaustive search—a complete search that covers everything current and past that was ever concerned with the subject under investigation.

extract—direct quotations from material, indicating the contents.

false drop—in a mechanized information storage and retrieval system, material that is not pertinent to the subject being investigated, but that is included along with the pertinent material. Also referred to as **noise.**

feedback—information provided to a manual or mechanized system which enables the system to react so as to maintain its operations or adapt them more closely to the needs of its users.

hard copy—the original document or a duplicate of it which can be read as is without special equipment.

hit—in a mechanized information storage and retrieval system, pertinent material that is retrieved.

indexing—selecting words and terms to identify the contents of informational material so that the data may later be located by anyone using these words or terms.

information center—a location where information is acquired, organized, analyzed, synthesized, stored, and disseminated for the needs of its customers.

information explosion—a term used to describe the exponential growth of information.

information scouting—locating unpublished material and keeping aware of who is working on what projects at what location.

information specialist—one who analyzes, synthesizes, and summarizes the contents of documents and who specializes in a particular subject. Sometimes referred to as a **literature research analyst.**

in-line processing—processing data as put into the system, without presorting or batching.

interest profile—the words or terms that describe an individual's field of interest.

key word—a significant word extracted from a document which is used to index the document.

KWIC—key-word-in-context; an index wherein each key word in the title of the document is used as an indexing term and is shown in its relationship to the other words in the title.

library—an organized collection of books, documents, etc.; the facilities to house the collection; and the personnel to maintain the collection for education, information, and recreation of patrons.

library loan program—an interlibrary program for the borrowing and lending of informational material.

library, special—an organization that acquires, organizes, maintains, utilizes, and disseminates the information material germane to the organization's activities.

Library of Congress classification—an alphanumeric classification method in which all knowledge is divided into 21 groups, designed for very large collections that require detailed subdivisions and expansion.

literature research analyst. See **information specialist.**

literature search—a complete review of all current and past published information relating to the subject of the inquiry, culminating with a list of abstracts of the pertinent information uncovered.

loan period—the amount of time that material may be borrowed.

management by exception—reporting only those items (good or bad) which deviate from the normal mode of operation.

microfiche—a 4″ x 6″ sheet of microfilm usually containing copies of 58 standard 8½″ x 11″ pages; any sheet of microfilm.

microfilm—a continuous roll of film containing microreproductions of original material.

microform—any facsimile of material that is reduced in physical size so as to require special equipment to view it, as in the case of microfiche, microfilm, and aperture cards.

miss—in an information storage and retrieval system, the relevant information that was not retrieved.

negative information—information that is not actually used in solving a problem, but that must be uncovered in order to determine what information is actually needed.

network—in PERT, a graphic representation of a plan.

noise. See **false drop.**

on-line processing—in direct contact with the central processing unit of a computer.

optical coincidence system—visual observation of the logical intersection of punched-out areas on cards. See **peekaboo card system.**

passive reference service—an information center service that provides the user with the tools for conducting his own search.

peekaboo card system—a method by which each indexing term is represented by a card and each document containing information about that term is allocated a specific punched hole in the card. When two or more of the indexing term cards are aligned, only those documents that contain all the terms will allow light to pass through the holes. Sometimes referred to as an **optical coincidence system.**

permuted index. See **KWIC.**

PERT—program evaluation and review technique; a technique for measuring and controlling development progress as regards time, cost, and performance.

pertinent information—information which specifically fulfills the need. See **relevant information.**

positive information—information that is relevant and pertinent to the problem.

presort—to arrange punched cards into large groups of similar items; the first stage in the sorting process.

probability of error—the chance that a mistake will be made. See **degree of risk.**

Project Lex—a joint government and industry venture in preparing a thesaurus.

punched card—a tabulating card into which are punched holes, representing coded information, for mechanized manipulation. Unlike edge-punched cards, the holes are punched in the body of the card.

real time—in a computerized system, the ability to process data at the time of occurrence for immediate use in problem solving and decision making. Information is constantly updated as new facts become available.

recall—those items retrieved from a store of information that are in some degree related to the sought-after information.

reference material—a collection of standard tools, such as mathematical tables and encyclopedias, used to locate information, as opposed to the literature covering the subject area.

reference service—the activity of a special library or information center that provides factual answers to its users without requiring user participation in searching for the material.

referral—informing users as to the best source from which to acquire needed information.

relevant information—retrieved information that is directly related to the question being asked.

research with information—solving a technical problem with recourse only to information rather than experimentation.

selective dissemination of information (SDI)—matching an individual's interest profile against new material entering the information center and automatically informing him of the availability of the information.

sigma system—a total management and technical information program that is based on summing up information for various levels of management; encompasses a clearinghouse concept in its approach.

slack time—in PERT, the difference between the time within which a project is expected to be completed and the time within which it is scheduled to be completed.

systems approach—determining the best method of accomplishing an objective within the imposed constraints of time, money, and material.

thesaurus—a listing of terms which are authorized to be used in an information storage and retrieval system. The conceptual relationships of the various terms are shown, and definitions are given when necessary.

time sharing—the simultaneous use of a computer by several users. As a rule, none of the users has to wait to use the computer, and there is no interference with the programs of others.

universal decimal classification—an expansion of the Dewey decimal classification system permitting more minute subdivisions. Also called the **Brussels classification.**

U.S. Patent Office classification—an arrangement of patents in groups according to subject matter. There are more than 300 main groupings, called classes, each of which is identified by a number and title. The 300 major classes are further broken down into 60,000 subclasses also identified by numbers and more specific titles.

word level indexing—indexing by words or terms as opposed to concepts.

Selected Bibliography

BOOKS

Becker, Joseph, and Robert M. Hayes, *Information Storage and Retrieval: Tools, Elements, Theories,* John Wiley & Sons, Inc., New York, 1963.

Bennett, William R., and J. R. Davey, *Data Transmission,* McGraw-Hill Book Company, Inc., New York, 1965.

Bourne, Charles P., *Methods of Information Handling,* John Wiley & Sons, Inc., New York, 1963.

Buckingham, Walter, *Automation: Its Impact on Business and People,* Mentor Executive Library Books, New York, 1963.

Burck, Gilbert, and the editors of *Fortune, Computer Age and Its Potential for Management,* Harper & Row, Publishers, Inc., New York, 1965.

Dearden, John, and F. W. McFarlan, *Management Information Systems —Text and Cases,* Richard D. Irwin, Inc., Homewood, Illinois, 1966.

Desmonde, William H., *Computers and Their Uses,* Prentice-Hall, Inc., Englewood Cliffs, New Jersey, 1964.

Elias, A. W., editor, *Technical Information Center Administration,* Spartan Books, Washington, D.C., 1964.

Elliott, C. O., and Robert S. Wasley, *Business Information Processing Systems,* Richard D. Irwin, Inc., Homewood, Illinois, 1965.

Fairthorne, R. A., *Towards Information Retrieval,* Butterworth & Company, Ltd., London, 1961.

Greenberger, Martin, editor, *Management and the Computer of the Future,* M.I.T. Press and John Wiley & Sons, Inc., New York, 1962.

Hattery, Lowell H., and Edward M. McCormick, editors, *Information Retrieval Management,* American Data Processing, Inc., Detroit, Michigan, 1963.

Head, Robert V., *Real-Time Business Systems,* Holt, Rinehart and Winston, Inc., New York, 1964.

Howard, James H., *Electronic Information Displays for Management,* American Data Processing, Inc., Detroit, Michigan, 1966.

Howerton, P. W., *Information Handling: First Principles,* Spartan Books, Washington, D.C., 1963.

Jonker, Frederick, *Indexing Theory, Indexing Methods and Search Devices,* Scarecrow Press, Inc., New York, 1964.

Kast, Fremont, and James Rosenzweig, editors, *Science, Technology, and Management,* McGraw-Hill Book Company, Inc., New York, 1963.

Kochen, Manfred, *Some Problems in Information Science,* Scarecrow Press, Inc., New York, 1965.

Licklider, J. C. R., *Libraries of the Future,* M.I.T. Press, Cambridge, Massachusetts, 1965.

Martino, Rocco L., *Project Management and Control,* 3 volumes, American Management Association, Inc., New York, 1964.

McDonough, Adrian M., *Information Economics and Management Systems,* McGraw-Hill Book Company, Inc., New York, 1963.

McDonough, Adrian M., and L. J. Garrett, *Management Systems,* Richard D. Irwin, Inc., Homewood, Illinois, 1965.

Meacham, Alan D., and others, editors, *Total Systems,* American Data Processing, Inc., Detroit, Michigan, 1963.

Nelson, C. E., *Microfilm Technology: Engineering and Related Fields,* McGraw-Hill Book Company, Inc., New York, 1965.

Prince, Thomas R., *Information Systems for Management Planning and Control,* Richard D. Irwin, Inc., Homewood, Illinois, 1966.

Smith, Paul T., *How to Live with Your Computer,* American Management Association, Inc., New York, 1965.

Solomon, Irving I., and L. O. Weingart, *Management Uses of the Computer,* Harper & Row, Publishers, Inc., New York, 1966.

Strauss, Lucille J., Irene M. Strieby, and Alberta L. Brown, *Scientific and Technical Libraries: Their Organization and Administration,* Interscience Publishers, Inc., New York, 1964.

Vickery, B. C., *On Retrieval System Theory,* 2nd edition, Butterworth & Co., London, 1965.

Wiesner, J. B., *Where Science and Politics Meet,* McGraw-Hill Book Company, Inc., New York, 1965.

PERIODICALS

"Automatic Message Switching and Processing System Utilized by Airline," *Journal of Machine Accounting, Data Processing Systems & Management,* Vol. 15, November 1964.

Baker, D. B., and M. Hosek, "Soviet Science Information Services," *Chemical and Engineering News*, Vol. 38, January 11, 1960.

Beckett, J. A., "Management, Motivation, and Management Information Systems," *Advanced Management Journal*, Vol. 30, January 1965.

Bello, Francis, "How to Cope with Information," *Fortune*, Vol. 62, September 1960.

Bement, K. T., "Toward Complete Management Information Systems," *Systems & Procedures Journal*, Vol. 14, September 1963.

Birmingham, Donald J., "Planning for Data Communications," *Data Processing Magazine*, Vol. 6, October 1964.

Boyd, D. F., and H. S. Krasnow, "Economic Evaluation of Management Information Systems," *IBM Systems Journal*, Vol. 2, March 1963.

Breen, John, "Managing the Information Flow," *Administrative Management*, Vol. 26, September 1965.

Burlingame, John F., "Information Technology and Decentralization," *Harvard Business Review*, Vol. 39, November–December 1961.

Bush, Vannevar, "As We May Think," *Atlantic Monthly*, Vol. 76, August 1945.

Caleo, R. L., "Retrieving What Your Firm Files: Special Report," *Administrative Management*, Vol. 24, August 1963.

Camilli, L. F., "Technical Unification in a Management Information System," *Management Accounting*, Vol. 47, April 1966.

Carter, N. H., and S. W. Kessler, "Management Information Systems," *Banking*, Vol. 58, May 1966.

Cary, F. T., "Computer Changes Management Art," *Iron Age*, Vol. 195, January 7, 1965.

"Central U.S. Data Center Idea Defended," *Electronic News*, Vol. 11, August 1, 1966.

"Computer Runs Show at Olin: Blueprint of a Total Information System," *Steel*, Vol. 156, June 28, 1965.

Culliton, James W., "Diagram of Management Control," *Harvard Business Review*, Vol. 38, March–April 1960.

Daniel, D. Ronald, "Management Information Crisis," *Harvard Business Review*, Vol. 39, September–October 1961.

"Data Retrieval: Management's Defense Against Waste," *Supervisory Management*, Vol. 8, August 1963.

Dearden, John, "Can Management Information Be Automated?" *Harvard Business Review*, Vol. 42, March–April 1964.

Dearden, John, "How to Organize Information Systems," *Harvard Business Review*, Vol. 39, March–April 1961.

Dearden, John, "Myth of Real-Time Management Information," *Harvard Business Review*, Vol. 44, May–June 1966.

Diebold, John, "ADP—The Still-Sleeping Giant," *Harvard Business Review,* Vol. 42, September–October 1964.

Duke, William F., "Information System Automation—Good or Bad?" *Computers & Data Processing,* Vol. 1, January 1964.

Dykeman, Frank C., "New Techniques for a Management Information System," *Financial Executive,* Vol. 34, March 1966.

Ehrle, R. A., "Implications of a Systems Approach to Organization and Management," *Personnel Journal,* Vol. 44, February 1965.

"Electronic Browsing," *Sales Management,* Vol. 93, October 16, 1964.

Elliott, J. R., Jr., "Information Please: Retrieving It from Today's Mass of Documents and Data Is a Demanding Task," *Barron's,* Vol. 44, October 19, 1964.

Evans, Marshall K., and Lou R. Hague, "Master Plan for Information Systems," *Harvard Business Review,* January–February 1962.

Fellowes, John, "Records Storage Cost Analysis," *Systems,* May 1966.

Fiock, L. R., Jr., "Seven Deadly Dangers in EDP," *Harvard Business Review,* Vol. 40, May–June 1962.

Fisch, G. G., "Integrated Management Organization," *Financial Executive,* Vol. 32, May 1964.

Frutkin, Arnold W., "International Cooperation in Space Research," *Astronautics and Aerospace Engineering,* March 1963.

Furth, S. E., "Mechanized Information Storage and Retrieval Made Easy," *Special Libraries,* Vol. 54, November 1963.

Galloy, Thomas A., "The Key to On-Line Systems," *Journal of Data Management,* Vol. 2, July 1964.

Garrity, John T., "The Management Information Dream: The End or a New Beginning?" *Financial Executive,* Vol. 32, September 1964.

Gentle, Edgar C., Jr., "Keeping Management Up to the Minute," *Computers & Data Processing,* Vol. 1, May 1964.

Guest, L. C., Jr., "Meeting the Challenge of Information Systems," *Financial Executive,* Vol. 34, August 1966.

Hague, L. R., "Better Management Information Systems," *The Office,* Vol. 59, January 1964.

Head, Robert V., "Programming the Real-Time System," *Journal of Data Management,* Vol. 2, February 1964.

Hertz, D. B., "Developing a Computerized Management Information System," *Management Review,* Vol. 55, April 1966.

"How Do You Keep Informed?" *Dun's Review and Modern Industry,* Vol. 85, May 1965.

"Information Becomes a Hot Item," *Business Week,* May 14, 1966.

Jacobs, Robert C., "Central Data System Tightens Management Control," *Journal of Machine Accounting, Data Processing Systems & Management*, Vol. 15, April 1964.

James, Glennon J., "Planning a Communication-Based Management Information System," *Computers and Automation*, Vol. 13, October 1964.

Kaimann, R. A., "Management by Exception Hierarchically," *Data Processing Magazine*, Vol. 8, July 1966.

"Keeping Ahead on Real Time," *Business Week*, March 27, 1965.

Klein, H. E., "Information Explosion in the Factory," *Dun's Review and Modern Industry*, Vol. 85, March 1965.

Kleinschord, W. A., "Finding the Information Retrieval System for You," *Administrative Management*, Vol. 26, April 1965.

Konkel, Paul E., "Management Information Systems Can Be Computerized," *Computers & Data Processing*, Vol. 1, June 1964.

"Learning to Live with Literature Explosions: Systematic Revolution in Reshaping Concepts of Scientific Information Storage and Retrieval," *Chemical Week*, Vol. 95, July 18, 1964.

Limberg, H., "Organization and the Management Information System," *The Office*, Vol. 60, July 1964.

Luhn, H. P., "Key-Word-In-Context Index for Technical Literature (KWIC Index)," *American Documentation*, Vol. 11, October 1960.

"Managing Information More Efficiently Through Consolidation," *Printers' Ink*, Vol. 46, January 22, 1965.

Mapletoft, J. T., "Satisfying the Need to Know in Real Time," *Systems & Procedures Journal*, Vol. 16, March 1965.

"Marketing Intelligence Systems: A Distant Early Warning Line for Marketing Men," *Business Management*, Vol. 29, January 1966.

Martino, Rocco L., "Creating the Integrated Management System," *Computers & Data Processing*, Vol. 1, April 1964.

Martino, Rocco L., "Development and Installation of a Total Management Information System," *Data Processing for Management*, April 1963.

Medin, A. C., "Cities Share Information Storage Techniques: Metropolitan Data Center Project," *Public Management*, Vol. 47, April 1965.

Menkus, B., "Information Systems in Marketing," *Systems & Procedures Journal*, Vol. 14, July 1963.

Meschamp, George M., "The Emerging Philosophy of Systems Management," *Journal of Data Management*, Vol. 2, October 1964.

"Meshing Managers and Computers: Deering Milliken's New Total Information Center," *Business Week*, July 3, 1965.

"NASA Speeds Technical Fallout to Industry," *Steel,* Vol. 158, April 4, 1966.

Newton, J. O., "Total System," *Management Accounting,* Vol. 47, July 1966.

"Objectives and Standards for Special Libraries," *Special Libraries,* December 1964.

Peck, D., "Automated Record Keeping," *Administrative Management,* Vol. 27, April 1966.

Porter, J. H., "What Management Should Know About Real-Time Systems," *Management Review,* Vol. 53, November 1964.

Ream, Norman J., "On-Line Management Information, Part 1," *Datamation,* Vol. 10, March 1964.

Ream, Norman J., "On-Line Management Information, Part 2," *Datamation,* Vol. 10, April 1964.

Redmond, D., "Small Technical Libraries: A Brief Guide to Their Organization and Operation," *UNESCO Bulletin for Libraries,* March–April 1964.

Romnes, H. I., "Managing the Information Revolution," *Bankers Monthly,* Vol. 83, July 1966.

Senensieb, N. L., "Management Information Crisis," *The Office,* Vol. 61, January 1965.

Smith, A. W., "How EDP Is Affecting Middle Management," *Administrative Management,* May 1966.

"Sophisticated Uses for Computers: Total Management Information System," *Business Management,* Vol. 27, October 1964.

Spindel, P. D., "Computer Based Management Information System," *Industrial Development and Manufacturers Record,* Vol. 134, January 1965.

Strassmann, P. A., "Forecasting Considerations in Design of Management Information Systems," *National Association of Accountants Bulletin,* Vol. 46, February 1965.

Stringfield, H., Jr., "How Automation Aids Management," *The Office,* Vol. 59, January 1964.

"There's Money in Memory: Management Is Finding that It Can Cut Down Sharply on Information Retrieval Costs," *Dun's Review and Modern Industry,* Vol. 82, September 1963.

Thurston, Philip H., "Who Should Control Information Systems?" *Harvard Business Review,* Vol. 40, November–December 1962.

"Toward a National Information System," *Special Libraries,* Vol. 56, July–August 1965.

Tuthill, O. W., "Thrust of Information Technology on Management," *Financial Executive,* Vol. 34, January 1966.

Veyette, J. H., Jr., "Information Retrieval Systems," *Systems,* Vol. 7, July 1966.

Wallin, H. N., "How the Navy Operates Its Management Information Center," *The Office,* Vol. 63, January 1966.

Weill, P., "Are You Ready for a Company Library?" *Administrative Management,* Vol. 24, August 1963.

Williams, Walter, F., "The Growing Data Volume—Can It Be Mastered?" *Business Automation,* Vol. 10, November 1963.

Winter, C. F., "Peripheral Data Processing: Its Contribution to Management Systems," *Systems & Procedures Journal,* Vol. 14, September 1963.

MISCELLANEOUS

Advances in EDP and Information Systems, Management Report 62, American Management Association, Inc., New York, 1961.

Advances in Management Information Systems Techniques, Management Bulletin 16, American Management Association, Inc., New York, 1962.

Bershadskiy, R. Y., *Vchenyy Kotoryy Znaet Vse,* (Soviet Developments in Information Storage and Retrieval) , Moscow, 1962, Evaluation by U.S. Department of Commerce, 1963.

Computer-Based Management for Information and Control, Management Bulletin 30, American Management Association, Inc., New York, 1963.

Control Through Information, Management Bulletin 24, American Management Association, Inc., New York, 1963.

Engineers Joint Council, *Thesaurus of Engineering Terms,* New York, May 1964.

"The Information Revolution," *The New York Times,* May 23, 1965.

Little, Arthur D., Inc., *Centralization and Documentation,* 2nd edition, Arthur D. Little, Inc., Cambridge, Massachusetts, June 1964.

President's Science Advisory Committee, *Improving the Availability of Scientific and Technical Information in the United States,* December 1958.

President's Science Advisory Committee, *Science, Government, and Information: The Responsibilities of the Technical Community and the Government in the Transfer of Information,* January 1963.

U.S. Congress, House of Representatives, Committee on Education and Labor, Hearings of the Ad Hoc Subcommittee on H. R. 1946, *National Information Center,* 88th Congress, 1st Session, Washington, D.C., May 1963.

U.S. Congress, House of Representatives, Committee on Government Operations, *Automatic Data Processing Equipment,* 89th Congress, 1st Session, Washington, D.C., March 1965.

U.S. Congress, House of Representatives, Committee on Government Operations, Select Committee on Government Research Report on H. R. 504, *Documentation and Dissemination of Research and Development Results,* 88th Congress, 2nd Session, Washington, D.C., November 1964.

U.S. Congress, Senate, Committee on Government Operations, *Report to the President on the Management of Automatic Data Processing in the Federal Government,* 89th Congress, 1st Session, Senate Document No. 15, Washington, D.C., March 1965.

U.S. Congress, Senate, Committee on Government Operations, *Summary of Activities Toward Interagency Coordination,* Report No. 369, 89th Congress, 1st Session, Washington, D.C., June 1965.

U.S. Department of Congress, *Scientific and Technological Communication in Government,* Washington, D.C., 1962.

U.S. National Aeronautics and Space Administration, *The Scientific and Technical Information Program of the National Aeronautics and Space Administration,* Washington, D.C., April 1962.

Index

Soviet-Bloc Research in Geophysics, Astronomy and Space, 129
Special Libraries Association, 51, 70, 90, 129; quoted 19
   directory of scientific translations, 70
   membership dues, 90
   Translations Center, 129
Special library, 19–20
Staff translator, requirements for, 70
Stegmaier, Dr. Robert B., Jr., quoted 130
Subject specialists, responsibilities of, 117
Summarization of information, 62–63
Supplies, cost of, 90
Symposium preprints, 74
Synthesis of information, 62–63
Systems approach to information, 40–56
Systems specialist, information, 112–113

T

Tapes, magnetic, 109–110
Tapes, paper, 109
Task plans in sigma system, 121
Technical Abstract Bulletin, 89, 130
Technical information specialists. *See* Literature research analysts
Technical personnel, information challenge to, 22–23
Technical summary progress reports, 123–124
Technical Translations, 70, 129
Thermophysical Properties Research Center, Purdue University, 130
Thesaurus, defined, 83
Thesaurus of Engineering Terms, 51, 83
Thomas' Register of American Manufacturers, 88
Time as constraint in closing information gap, 34–35
Timeliness of information, 93–94
Top management information, 25
Tough-Minded Management, 41
Transcriptions of meetings, 74
Translations, 64, 70
   cost of, 89
   scientific, directory of, 70
Translations Center, Special Libraries Association, 129

Translator, staff, requirements for, 70
Transmittal of information, methods of, 29, 31
Travel expenses, cost of, 90
Tufts University Human Engineering Information and Analysis Service, 130

U

United Engineering Trustees, 126
   Engineering Societies Library, 126
United Nations Educational, Scientific, and Cultural Organization (UNESCO), 132
U.S. Department of Labor, 128
U.S. Government Printing Office, 70, 89, 128
   Monthly Catalog of United States Government Publications, 128
   Selected United States Government Publications, 73, 128
U.S. Government Research and Development Reports, 89, 129
U.S. Patent Office, 47, 73
   Gazette, 73
Universal decimal classification system, 47
User orientation, 75–76, 99–101
User services, external, 63
User survey, 100
USSR Abstracts, 129

V

Vseseyusnyy Institut Nauchney i Teknicheskey Informatsii (VINITI), 133
   Ekspress Informatsiya, 133
   Itegi Nauki, 133
   Referativny Zhurnal, 133

W

Wages and salaries, 87
Weinberg, Dr. Alvin M., 127
Wilde, Oscar, quoted 99
Wilson Company, H. W., 73, 88
   Business Periodicals Index, 73, 88
   Readers' Guide to Periodical Literature, 73, 88
Wilson Library Bulletin, quoted 22